Praise For Fall In Love With Your Flawsomeness

As I read through this book, the vulnerability and rawness with which Barb shares her story, felt so real, that at times I felt like I was reading something about myself. Her writing and the way she shares her life's journey gives the reader a constant undercurrent of hope, of how love and compassion are an inside job!

—**Lynne Milne,**
Metaphysical Healer and author

Barb finds ways to convert her past pain into a bridge for others to cross, where they can find relief from the pain and trauma of their own pasts. This book is that bridge.

—**Alvin Brown Life Coach**
and Best-Selling Author of *Journey to Personal Greatness: Mind, Body and Soul. A Blueprint for Life Balance and Self Mastery*

This book will have you smiling through your tears and yearning for more from this wonderful, wonderful woman.

—**Elissa Lowenstern,**
author of *Making the Impossible, Possible*

This book is not only captivating but exceptionally well written, transforming to the heart, mind and soul. I haven't read a book this well written and with such presence in a very long time.

—**Sindy Gumby Zemura,**
Founder & CEO of Southern Africa Embrace Foundation

Barbs journey from trauma to transformation illustrates that even in the most trying circumstances, we can rise and fully embody the strength inside each and every one of us. Her story is powerful, but the person she has become as a result of her experiences is even more so.

—**Codi Shewan,**
author of *Every Legacy,
Lessons for Living with Purpose Right Now*

Fall in Love with Your *Flawsomeness:*

Healing and Transforming
the Wounds of Trauma to Create
Your Exceptional Life

By
Barbara Takeda

Soul Full Expressions

Copyright © 2022 Barbara Takeda

All rights reserved. The use of any part of this publication, reproduced, transmitted in any form or by any means electronic, mechanical, photocopying, recording, or otherwise, or stored in a retrieval system without the prior written consent of the author/publisher— or in the case of photocopying or other reprographic copying, license from the Canadian Copyright Licensing agency—is an infringement of the copyright law.

ISBN Hardcover: 978-1-7777732-2-9
ISBN Paperback: 978-1-7777732-0-5
ISBN e-Book: 978-1-7777732-1-2

Text design by Amit Dey
Cover design by Barbara Takeda
Published in Canada by Soul Full Expressions
www.barbaratakeda.ca

Dedicated to

SB: I had to suffer losing you to find myself

Table of Contents

Foreword by Elissa Lowenstern xi

Introduction xv
    Poem: Exceptional Woman xvi
    Poem: Coming Home xxii

Chapter One: Crushed Bit by Bit 1
    Exceptional Woman Challenge – MEDITATION 18

Chapter Two: Looking for Love in All the Wrong Places. 21
    Exceptional Woman Challenge: LOOK INTO YOUR
        VALUE. 34

Chapter Three: The Computer Age 35
    Exceptional Woman Challenge: SURRENDER AND
        ACCEPTANCE 41

Chapter Four: A Fresh Start 43
    Exceptional Woman Challenge: YOU DONE GOOD!. . . . 47

Chapter Five: Gains & Losses 49
    Exceptional Woman Challenge: BE IN CONTROL
        OF YOUR DASH. 54

Chapter Six: Pain and Deception. 55
    Exceptional Woman Challenge: FORGIVENESS 61

Chapter Seven:: Secrets and Lies 63
    Exceptional Woman Challenge: SELF CARE & SELF LOVE . . 67

Chapter Eight: Finding my Health Again 69
    Exceptional Woman Challenge: FROM LACK
        TO ABUNDANCE. 72

Chapter Nine: Profound Loss 73
    Exceptional Woman Challenge: GROWING THROUGH
        GRIEF AND LOSS. 86

Chapter Ten: Coming Home. 87
    Exceptional Woman Challenge: USING THE POWER
        OF ENERGY TO HEAL 94

Chapter Eleven: Understanding the Lessons Underlying Loss . . . 95
    Exceptional Woman Challenge: RECOGNIZING TRUE
        AND AUTHENTIC RELATIONSHIPS 100

Chapter Twelve: Gratitude: The Catalyst that Changed my Life . 101
    Exceptional Woman Challenge: PRACTICING
        GRATITUDE DAILY 106

Chapter Thirteen: Clean up Your Life & Your Space. 107
    Exceptional Woman Challenge: CREATE HARMONY
        IN YOUR LIFE. 110

Chapter Fourteen: You CAN Rewrite Your Life 111

    Exceptional Woman Challenge: ACCEPT THAT EVERYTHING IS ALWAYS PERFECTLY PERFECT 117

Chapter Fifteen: Exploring Emotions Through Poetry 119

Additional Resources 131

Gratitudes. 133

About the Author 135

Foreword

Barb and I have never met in person. In fact, we live almost ten thousand miles from one another; yet, when I read her extraordinary book, *Fall in Love with Your Flawsomeness: Healing and Transforming the Wounds of Trauma to Create Your Exceptional Life*, I felt Barb's journey with every fibre of my being. Her poetry sent shivers through my body, not only because we share lived experiences of abuse and illness—experiences of utter desperation and despair that we no longer wanted to be alive—but also because we both made a choice to heal. It is through self-healing that we were led to help others to heal.

I was first drawn to Barb a few years ago on social media. I was in awe of her raw honesty—her seamless ability to share so generously from her heart in a public forum. This is something that doesn't come easily for many of us. As both someone who has advocated for and legally represented victims of childhood sexual abuse and as a practitioner of several modalities spanning many years, I feel truly humbled to sit at the feet of such an incredible woman.

This book is an invitation from the heart. It is Barb's deepest wish that her writing be used as a healing tool. Whether you are yet to embark on your healing journey and are wanting to be inspired and given a gentle nudge, or whether you would like to delve deeply into

Barb's treasure-chest of healing jewels and modalities. This book helps you to use Barb's experience and teachings as a guide, as a lighthouse is to ships in the night. Perhaps you want to just walk alongside Barb and experience the beauty, the sorrow, the courage, and the wisdom with which she pens the brilliantly woven tapestry of her life. That is okay too. For us, she connects her life of abuse and control, of loss and tragedy, of illness and injury, all of which leads towards a life of compassion and empathy, love and forgiveness, and joy and serenity.

There were times during her story when I couldn't hold back my tears. The vision of a small child, a child that always tried to please her parents, a good girl who knew her Bible well, who was wearing her favourite dress while bending over a fake-leather, yellow chair waiting for a beating from her father. This beating, one of many, was so severe it left that dress in tatters and it could never be worn again. But then Barb lifted me up again, as she does so well throughout her book. She lifted me up and put me down gently in the present, where she expressed her learnings as a lesson and I gained wisdom from her description of her healing. As she states: "A star need darkness to shine."

The book is brimming with exercises, daily rituals, steps on how to use various healing modalities, insights, and a unique perspective from a woman who once hated herself and her body. Barb describes her transformation to a woman who embraced her wounded inner child, held that child in her arms, told her she was enough and that she was okay. Barb was in her fifties when she became determined to find the courage, the determination, and the perseverance to heal herself physically and emotionally.

Nowadays, Barb's list of accomplishments is bountiful. She is a best-selling motivational author, a co-author of *The Courage to Change*. Barb is a Reiki master healer, speaker, spiritual mentor, and a coach. She encourages and inspires women to embrace their greatness using the same tools that she employed to turn her own pain into wisdom. Born out of her connection with her soul, Barb's company, Soul Full

Expressions, offers a signature event, "An Exceptional Woman" —a place where women come to be inspired and empowered.

Falling in Love with My Flawsomeness is timed perfectly and is important to the foundation of public discourse. Written against a backdrop of the COVID-19 pandemic and climate change discourse, her words sum up the time: a time when countries around the world are facing so many difficult and divisive challenges. A time when people are struggling with their mental wellbeing, when fear and anger have been acutely felt and expressed. She is writing for these times and yours if you find the book in the future. At times, we all need a beacon of light, a place to find hope and the stuff that dreams are made of.

I hope you enjoy this wondrous book as much as I have. This book will have you smiling through your tears and yearning for more from this wonderful, wonderful woman.

Elissa Lowenstern
January 2022

Introduction

Is your life everything you want? Can you express gratitude for everything—good or bad—in your life? Can you look in the mirror, into your own eyes and say, "I love you," and mean it? Do you struggle to cope with difficulties, find losses unbearable, and are unable to get over past traumas? If you want to live life with a calmness that is your understanding that everything is always perfectly perfect and given to you to aid you in becoming the exceptional person you are destined to be, then this book is definitely for you.

Until I was in my late fifties, I lived most of my life in great physical pain accompanied by inner turmoil that was sometimes worse. I was angry and resentful at the world, and I was not listening to the messages my body was constantly giving me. Pain is a messenger, telling you that something is off, your emotional vibrations are too low, you're holding onto something that needs healing and release.

When my journey with chronic pain began, I'd simply pop a painkiller, but over the years as I was diagnosed with numerous auto-immune diseases, it wasn't very long until I was taking over one dozen prescriptions and self-injecting prescribed narcotics for my chronic pain. I was oblivious to the very strong messages embedded in my pain. And, despite a life surrounded by people who regularly told me,

"I love you," I felt lonely and unloved. But ever so gently throughout the past decade, as I have worked diligently to heal my life, I found myself shifting. I experienced a major change in my consciousness and for the first time in my life, I heard and felt profound and deep love from my soul.

None of us gets through life without some trauma; it is how you deal with what life throws at you that makes the difference. Growing up, I felt ugly, and that is what I saw when I looked at myself in the mirror. I was sexually assaulted in my late teens, I survived countless miscarriages, and underwent several unnecessary surgeries performed by a negligent doctor leaving me with permanent physical and emotional injuries that wracked my body with pain.

My past traumas, abuse, and losses were so numerous that I believed these were all proof I was a worthless human being. Through attention to my emotional health and release of what no longer served me, I was able to radically reframe this view of myself. I was able to release my past so I could become the best version of myself.

It is my deepest desire that at the end of this book, you will speak these words with sincerity and from the love you hold in your heart for yourself.

I am an exceptional woman.

You might ask me why. Is it because I can articulate? Because I can motivate? Because I can elevate?

Are my hips too wide? Is it my luscious curves? Or the way I sashay?

Children should be seen and not heard.

Don't talk so loudly. Don't laugh so loud—it's not ladylike. Don't be so sensitive. You cry too much. We have no beauties in our family. We're just average.

So, I hid behind my shyness.

I looked in the mirror and saw less than average—freckles, scrawny body, braces, pigtails, orthopaedic shoes.

How would a boy ever like me?

Be modest they said, get married, have babies. And remember, he won't buy the cow if he gets the milk for free! Keep your man happy, be subservient.

Women must not speak in the church. Women cannot be a leader in the church. Cover and keep your head bowed. Learn bookkeeping and typing. You'll need them if you don't find a man.

My very worth and value depended on a man.

My worth and my value laid in my virginity. Being with a man before marriage is a sin. You must maintain your virginity for your husband!

So, I dimmed my light, I turned it down, I turned it off and I let it burn out. I withdrew and I silenced my voice.

Don't look at me. I'm nothing .... I'm not worthy .... I'm not deserving.

But then I learned that I was a toy.

Something for a man's pleasure. Something to be enjoyed and tossed away. My body was used, abused, and discarded.

Wide hipped, luscious, and curvy.

I am an exceptional woman.

I am filled with pure source energy. I challenge the structure of existing form as we know it. I am here to heal the earth and bring her back to a conscious awareness of a creative and spiritual power called the Divine feminine.

I am a force of natural radiance and I will not be stopped.

I do not crave material or external fixes for my security or my fulfillment. I have discovered and uncovered the magic that I was programmed to forget and disuse.

My wisdom lies in my body, my feelings, and in my never-ending flowing cycles of energy.

I immerse myself in stillness, where I find my home. Look deeply into my eyes and you will find yourself there.

After years of abuse, trauma, and suffering, I found my light! And I will NOT dim my light.

Does my light make you uncomfortable?

That only makes me shine bigger and brighter!

I will NOT sit down, I will not shut up, I will not turn it off or hide it away. I came here to love and to be loved! I love this luscious, too curvy, well padded, wide hipped woman's body. Because this temple is my soul's home.

My beauty rises in ways my cells do not yet understand. My body is luminous and ripe, carrying the weight of my passion.

I am an exceptional woman.

I will not shut-up, I will not sit down. And I will not be put in a corner ... baby.

I will embrace my luscious, well- upholstered body in all its divine glory! I will move my body with intention. I will speak with integrity and love. My heart is open and I love unconditionally and all inclusively. But do not mistake me for a fool! I can affect you with my energy.

Does my light make you uncomfortable?

That only makes me shine brighter!

*I am a too much woman ... I am an uncommon woman ...
I am a resilientista ... I am fearless ... I am one woman....
I am an exceptional woman!*

*And I WILL shine ... I WILL articulate ... I WILL elevate,
and ... I WILL motivate.*

Because I AM an exceptional woman.

I invite you to take this journey with me as I share my story. Come along with me as we dive into many of the beliefs, principles, and healing modalities I have embraced so that you, too, can begin your healing journey.

Life can be easy or hard. It is your choice.

I was fifty-seven when I had my moment, made my breakthrough, and began my journey to find the real, authentic Barb. It is my intention that what I share in this book helps you to switch from simply existing to joyfully living. I encourage you to be present in your life, enjoy the precious moments you have been given in your lifetime.

Do not waste your moments being a victim of your past.

When we dwell on the past, it prevents us from seeing the opportunities that are presenting themselves in each and every moment. When we hold on to anger and resentment, we remain rooted in the past, unable to feel genuine gratitude for what we have right now. When we worry, feel anxiety, or experience panic attacks, we are projecting ourselves into a future that is not yet ours; one that has not happened and most likely, will not.

**This tells the Universe that we are <u>NOT</u> trusting
our journey.**

It is possible to live a peaceful, abundant, and happy life. When we can stay rooted in the present moment, we can be at peace. I have provided you with Exceptional Woman Challenges, which you will find at the end of every chapter. I will lead the way so you can become the woman or man you were born to be.

The present moment is your gift – consider it "a present" and enjoy it!

Sailing the waters and staying firmly anchored in the present moment of your life can be overwhelming at first. However, do you know that you already have everything you need within you to heal? There is only one thing standing in your way, and that is you. So, get out of your own way and allow the Universe to give you everything you want and everything you deserve in this lifetime.

Throughout this book, I will provide you with gentle nudges showing you how.

Capturing my emotions through writing has been tremendously healing for me. If my words inspire you, that is my intention. It is my deepest desire that you find your passion, your purpose, and your light.

You will see as I share my story with you, that I move in and out of the past and my stories to the present by sharing the many lessons I've learned. I will introduce you to the healing modalities that have enabled me to come home, along with my methodology so that you can use them, too, as it is my purpose in life to inspire, motivate, and empower you to achieve and live your best possible life, and be the exceptional person you were intended to be.

As we begin our journey of healing, our own personal energetic vibrations begin to rise. Do you realize that your energetic vibrations reach far beyond your physical body? Have you ever walked into a room full of people and you feel uncomfortable? You are responding to someone else's energy. When others are continually in contact with us, our vibrations affect them, as they too begin their healing which in turn raises their vibration.

And this, my dear friends, is how we *will* heal the world.

I open my heart and extend my hand to you as I invite you to come along with me as I share my journey to become an Exceptional Woman. Becoming an Exceptional Woman allowed me to fall in love with every bit of me and know that, although flawed, I am enough—that I am flawsome. *(Flawsome—a word coined by Tyra Banks in 2014.)* Join me on this journey where I will describe and share my path to healing. It is my deepest wish that if you complete the exercises and Exceptional Woman Challenges that follow each chapter, it will lead you to your own healing. Each exercise is designed to give you the tools to help you release your past and claim your present. Your future will be determined by the steps you take now.

With love

Barb

Coming Home

The pain of the past, simmering just beneath the face she exposed to the world,
Always there, churning and bubbling - destroying her self-esteem, her morals, her thoughts, her abilities.
Deeper and deeper, she buried the pain, until she no longer recognized it.
What happened to this woman? What hurts, what pain, what grief left her wanting health, happiness, and freedom from the pain?
How deep must she dig to release this pain? Can she find what she seeks?
She experienced abuse, she experienced death, she experienced the sting of cruelty from friends, the bite of hate within her family. All working together to create that fertile ground for every negative emotion - anger, resentment, self-loathing, judgement, bitterness, envy.
This girl was good for no one.
But then one day her whole life changed. She was brought to the edge, but could she take the next step? What was waiting beyond?
Forgiveness, acceptance, self-love, humility:
All within her reach, yet was she ready to release the past?
The cloaks of grief and depression were wrapped tightly around her. They had her locked within their grips, they comforted her, they eased her pain, protected her from the world.
Was she ready to drop these crutches? No.
But deep within, she knew she must let them drop from her body as leaves must drop from the trees in autumn.
Shifting, awakening, changing at her core, releasing ego, piety, anger, resentments.

The list was painfully long. The pain was moving upwards and outwards—It was breaking the surface, wearing her down, reliving and reminding her of the trauma.

How low her vibrations were, but now they were rising. She felt the difference in her soul. She loved, she laughed, she was embracing the wholeness of life.

Reiki became part of her journey, introduced to her one winter solstice night. She felt the pulsing energy and knew she was home. Her searching was done. A new spiritual life was opening to her.

The fear of death was gone—replaced with peacefulness.

The horrors of a cruel God —replaced with a Divine source of unconditional love.

She pondered her lives, previously and yet to come. How many lives had she lived? How many more would she live? What gifts had she given, what gifts had yet she yet to offer the world?

A new life was hers – was within her reach. The hurts were all gone, replaced with unconditional and all-encompassing love. How did she exist unaware for so long unaware? Living but not living. Reiki had brought her this joy. She would be forever grateful for that winter solstice night when she felt the energy in that hand on her shoulder.

Waking her up, changing her core, filling her up.

She truly had come home.

Chapter One

Crushed Bit by Bit

*T*he little girl sat in the middle of the double bed that she shared with her younger sister. Her tattered dress was spread all around her as silent tears traced tracks down her cheeks. This time he had used the skipping rope. With each lash against her bare thighs, she felt his fury, but then slowly, tears formed at the corners of his eyes. He spoke quietly, saying, "This hurts me too, but this is the only way you will learn."

Her father was "a stern disciplinarian," and when her parents talked about other bad children, they blamed the parents. The girl heard them. She wanted to be good. She wanted to please her parents.

"Spare the rod, spoil the child." Her father, coming from a family of thirteen children, firmly believed and adhered to this line from a verse in the Bible. He also had been raised by a firm disciplinarian himself, one who many times disciplined his boys with a good punch in the face. It was what he knew. The girl had been raised to study and memorize the Bible. She knew the verse but wondered deep down was this what it meant? In the Bible, the verse in Proverbs says, "He who spares the rod hates his son, but he who loves him is careful to discipline him."

But she dared not speak her thoughts out loud.

As she sat, she wondered, what did she need to learn? She read and studied her Bible dutifully, endeavouring to do everything that her parents and other grownups said to do. The girl was ten years old and already she felt unworthy, unloved, and certainly not good enough. Her confidence and self-esteem had been shattered bit by bit with each whipping she received.

Her mother loved to sew mother/daughter dresses for the three girls of the family: one for herself, another for the girl, and a cute tiny one for the girl's little sister. After that day, the girl's matching dress was never again worn; it was left beyond repair after the whipping.

That little girl, as you have probably guessed, is me. The memory of this one whipping amongst so many others continue to haunt me, perhaps because of how much I loved that dress. It is one of my earliest childhood memories. When a spanking was to be delivered, my father would send me downstairs to his office. I was to bend over a large, armless yellow chair which was covered in artificial leather with one big button in the middle of the back.

How I hated that chair.

How often as a child, I heard, "if you don't stop crying, I'll give you something to cry about." I remember one particular time. I had a doll, Susie, that I loved. Her head came off, and I was devastated. I cried and cried and cried for my Susie. And of course, my dad threatened that he would give me something to cry about if I did not stop carrying on.

Too sensitive, too much, too emotional. Naturally, this conditioned me to learn to suppress my emotions. When we suppress our emotions, our original, true self is slowly put to death by the conditioning and programming from outside sources. We grow up believing that our ego is our true self and create our life built on false foundations. As children, we do have the ability to advocate for ourselves, so we surrender to the conditioning and programming we receive, which results in a separation between our true self and our essence, or who we truly are. We create a persona or archetype to ensure that our needs are met. The surrender is so gradual that we are not even aware of how we are slowly changing to fit into the mold that family and society demands. So, we grow up with a false sense of identity – a face which keeps us safe from the fear that we are unworthy and unlovable.

My parents bought the home I grew up in when I was three years old. A typical mid-century, suburban bungalow. My mother was a stay-at-home mom, and my father was a financial consultant. He was well established in his career, so we lacked for nothing. Our home always smelled faintly of Noxzema cream, which my mom used religiously on her skin, as well as Mennen's Skin Bracer, which my dad used after shaving. I can still see my dad patting Mennen's on his face after shaving while squeezing his eyes shut as it stung his freshly shaved skin. In the bathroom, there were always fresh new blue jars of Noxzema cream on the counter.

We were raised in a strict, religious home. My parents created an oasis there to encourage us to stay at home. I was not allowed to attend bowling alleys, pool halls, movies, or other social gatherings where, as my dad said, "sinners congregate." They gave us what they could to keep us home and happy: a pool in the back garden and a finished basement with state-of-the-art entertainment.

Our life revolved around the church. We attended services, two—sometimes three—times on Sundays, twice through the week for prayer meetings and Bible studies, and I went to Pioneer Girl's, a group similar to Girl Guides/Scouts but overseen by our religious organization. I can distinctly remember my father telling me that in his life, God came first, the church was second, my mom was third, and we, his children came fourth.

When my father married my mom, he was already a father of three children from his first marriage. My mother didn't think she was able to have children, so it was a pleasant surprise when I, the first child from their union, came along five years later. I was also the first grandchild for my mother's parents. My maternal grandfather, my "Gampie," doted on me.

My mom told me he used to carry me up and down the stairs on a pillow when I was a baby. He treated me like a china doll. This beautiful man was my rock, and I loved him like no other.

Sitting through long Sunday services was so much better when Gampie was beside me. He would always have small, hard, wrapped candies in his pocket, give me one and then take the wrapper, quietly smooth it out, fold it into thirds, then turn it and fold the long side once again into thirds. He would then take the folded wrapper, fold it thirds once more and twist each end in opposite directions, turning that simple wrapper into a wee bow tie. And do you know I still do the same with wrappers to this day—a sweet little remembrance of him.

Many of my happiest childhood memories are of times spent with my adored Gampie. He loved woodworking, and I remember sitting in his workshop, watching as he built yet another piece of furniture with his enormous collection of specialized tools, teaching me what each tool was used for. Lessons I've used to this day in many of my own home renovations.

I stayed over with my grandparents as often as I could, and as a very young girl, sitting on the bathroom counter, I loved to watch my Gampie as he performed his morning shaving ritual. Wide-eyed, I watched him methodically lathering up the soap in his shaving cup with a brush as the familiar clean scent of soap filled the room, a fragrance I always associated with Gampie. Then, he brushed the foamy soap evenly all over his cheeks, chin, and neck. Gently, he twisted open the wings on his razor, dropped in a straight blade, and then twisted the wings back down to safely contain the blade. He then carefully drew the blade down through the foamy soap on his face, removing the whiskers from his face and leaving a soap-free path indented in all the white. He would stop and let me feel how smooth his cheek was after his first few strokes, telling me, "This is how it should feel, clean and smooth".

Oh, how I adored this man. He was like a father to me, and I would give up anything to spend time with him. I can still see his face, hear his laughter and his beautiful tenor voice that occasionally slipped into a Gaelic/Welsh accent when he sang hymns in church. He had lost his teeth as a young man, so he had upper and lower dentures.

I remember him holding his denture in his hand and pointing to one tooth, "Barbi, this is the tooth I'm cleaning today". I grew up thinking that his other teeth must feel awful if he didn't clean them all every day. It took me a few years to figure out that he was only playing a joke on me. However, a lovely, joyous memory for me today of him.

I was an only child for nearly six years before my younger brother came along, and then three years after him, my younger sister was born. Because of the gap in our ages, I slowly, over the years became the family babysitter and protector of my younger siblings. I adored my younger brother and baby sister, walking them to school, always looking out for them, growing into the girl that my parents wanted me to be. As a girl, I learned to never think of myself but always of others first. I was taught that loving myself or thinking of myself was sinful. There was no pride or vanity allowed in our home. I can still hear my dad's booming voice saying, "Wearing nail polish – that was Jezebel's *(a Biblical character)* downfall".

Throughout these early years, I learned to be a people pleaser, never saying no, or speaking up for myself. *Good girls do what they were told.* This is truly the definition of a patriarchal family unit. Women born and raised into a patriarchal society, like I was, end up either extremely intelligent or sick with illness and disease—which as you will read was the future that was written for me.

When I was four years old, my parents bought a beautiful, brand new Heinzman upright grand piano and immediately started me in piano lessons. Although my younger brother and sister also took lessons, I dove into music and I exceled very quickly. Music and art were my world. When I sat down to practice, I disappeared into my music—Brahms, Mozart, Beethoven—they took me to another world.

This was a world where nothing but me and my music existed. Hours could tick by and I would take no notice of how long I'd been sitting at the piano playing, until something brought me back to reality. Most often, it was my bottom which got numb and very uncomfortable from sitting so long on that wooden bench. That beautiful instrument was mine.

I regularly cleaned and polished her, and I never had to be told to practice. She and I grew up together, she was mine and I was hers, heart, mind, and soul. I studied Royal Conservatory music and theory until I was sixteen, finishing with grade eight in music and intermediate level in theory. For so many years, as I grew older, my piano and I would escape into my music world where absolutely nothing could touch me, nothing could invade my space, and where I could lose myself in my music. She was my haven throughout the bullying, the whippings, the teasing. She was always waiting to whisk me away to our own perfect Narnia.

My music teacher lived in a subdivision not too far from us, which was within walking distance from my home. So once a week, on Thursdays after school, I packed up my music books and headed over to her home. After my lesson was over, I would head home, but every so often I would end up at my grandparent's home that just happened to be along the route to my music lessons. Their home always smelled like homemade cookies and often, I would arrive to Nannie's famous snickerdoodle cookies with bits of cherries in them. Nannie would set a place for me for dinner at their wee table in a corner of the kitchen where Gampie and I would sit munching on warm cookies, laughing and singing while Nannie got dinner ready. If I sit quietly enough today, I can still hear his beautiful laughter.

And singing—how I loved to sing! I joined the choir in my senior years of elementary school. I also loved Mrs. Lawrence, my most wonderful and beloved elementary school music teacher. She lived not far from me in my neighborhood and I would often go by her very bohemian and eclectic home, which was on a beautiful ravine, and we would sit in her garden sipping tea and chatting. How I loved her and how I loved to sing for her. We were entered into many Kiwanis festivals, always taking the top spot. Music was such a joy to me; I went on in my teens to create a trio with two other girls in my church. We traveled around many, many churches in the Toronto area, sharing our love of singing and music. However, as much as I loved my music, my proficiency in music could not save me from the eventual loss of my self-worth, self-esteem and self-love.

As I grew older, my sense of self-worth disappeared, falling lower and lower until I could no longer find it. Going through my pre-teen and teenage years was a painful experience. I always shied away from people because of my perceived belief that they thought so little of me, they were criticizing and judging me, or they were pitying me or making fun of me. I easily slipped into being an introvert due to my extreme self-consciousness. I dreamed that somewhere within me, there existed a perfect girl. I dreamt of one day waking up to her, this perfect girl who would have no glasses, a perfectly developing figure, no freckles, no orthopaedic shoes, perfect blonde hair, and blue eyes. The young men would cluster around her, vying for her attention, and she would have friends aplenty that loved and adored her. This perfect girl's life was easy. Where was she, and why couldn't I wake up and suddenly be her?

As I began to heal myself, I learned that the Perfect Woman was an elusive dream that I chased after due to my low self-esteem and hatred for myself. And, as you'll see in future chapters, once I began my healing journey, I found that I was the Perfect Woman, and came to love myself just as I am—a flawsome woman!

I continued to study and delve deeply into my own healing, devouring many books on toxic shame and how to heal the shame that binds us. I understand how shame and guilt become deeply engrained in us when physical punishment is used regularly. Every lash of a belt or a whip instills in us that we are inherently bad, while reinforcing that we must conform and comply to survive in this world.

As parents, it is imperative when disciplining our children that we impress on them that the action they took was bad and not that "they" are bad. How often have you heard a parent, when angry with their child, yell at them, "you are such a bad girl" or "you are such a naughty boy." This embeds shame in the child, which will manifest in later years in many different ways.

It is also important to be aware of the difference between shame and guilt. Shame has the person asking themselves, "What happened in my life that made me feel so worthless?" "What is wrong with me?" They believe there is something inherently wrong with them. Guilt, on the other hand, has them asking, "Why do I feel badly?" "What did I do, or what didn't I do, that I could have changed?" As you can see, there is a tremendous distance between shame and guilt. Within shame, the person inherently believes they are bad, however, with guilt, they believe they did something wrong and want to find a way to correct it.

Constant reminders of this through incorrect or inappropriate discipline begins to chip away at the self-love and self-esteem that we are born with, and then, this is where guilt and/or shame step in and fills up that gap. Guilt tells us we did something bad, and consistent reinforcement of that leads to shame. Shame tells us we *are* bad, which is why we do bad things.

A strong religious upbringing can also create shame through the programmed belief that we are born into original sin. I was taught that I came into this world unworthy and sinful, that I was a filthy creature. I was taught that only by the grace of God could I possibly be saved from an afterlife of eternal damnation, burning in the fires of hell. This was a belief that I struggled with throughout my entire life. Questions and contradictions raged in my own internal belief system as I was also taught that we are created in the image of God. How then can we be unworthy, sinful, filthy creatures if we are created in God's image and He is perfect?

Through various methods of programming and conditioning such as these, we are set up for a lifetime of guilt and shame that binds us to our past, pressing down deeper and deeper in our psyche until we eventually implode. Then our inner critic takes front and centre stage, judging ourselves and everyone else. When we judge others, we are seeing our own inadequacies and projecting them onto them and refusing to look at our own emotional shortfalls.

It is important to note here that we have no control over the programming and conditioning we were raised with. When we reach adulthood, it becomes our responsibility to overcome and heal whatever traumas, losses, and abuses we suffered as children. We can choose to heal, or we can choose to continue to stay the victim of our story.

Through my own healing, I can see that my father, like so many others —myself included —used humour as a shield to hide behind. It was the way he protected himself, building a protective wall of comedic reactions and responses, to prevent the world from seeing his vulnerability. I see this so often: a child who becomes the class clown, an adult who hides their vulnerability behind wisecracks, being the life of the party, maybe even doing stand-up comedy professionally. I recently spoke with a dear friend who told me he is a BIG people pleaser, but when wearing his comedic mask, he doesn't give a flying fig what others think of him. So, we create these alternate egos to deal with the circumstances that our inner child cannot handle. We tuck him or her away in a safe place and wear the comedic mask which protects us as we step into our adulthood. However, the problem with this is our inner child stays at the age where the damage first occurred and never gets healed unless we willingly and willfully step out of our comfort zone to embrace and heal our inner child.

In my family, my father was always the comedian, constantly picking on us, using comedy to neatly wrap up and present his critical comments. He always had fun as the practical joker of our family. Unfortunately, his many jokes were critical in nature. As a child, I was very thin and wore glasses, having what I considered millions of freckles, and problematic feet which required specialized, orthopedic shoes— paradoxically, the type that the kids today think are "dope" —Doc Martens. My dad took great delight in making everyone laugh by slinging his funny criticisms/comments at my siblings and me.

Barbi, you are so thin, if you drank a bottle of tomato juice, you'd look like a thermometer.

Barbi, you are so thin, if you stand sideways and stick out your tongue, you'd look like a zipper.

Barbi, if you got lost, they could stick a stamp on you and slide you right under the front door.

Barbi, you're so ugly, if someone picked you up, they'd drop you at the first lamppost when they took a look at you.

Although they generated much laughter from other family members, they cut deep and constantly chipped away at me, eroding my already delicate sense of self and what little self-worth and esteem that I had. There is an old saying, *"sticks and stones may break my bones, but words will never hurt me."* I call BS on this quote. Words are sharper than any two-edged razor. And, once said, they can never be taken back. When dealing with our children, or other relationships, we need to think carefully about the words we use with them. Do you sling accusatory words at your partner, your children? Do you never take the blame, but always look for someone else to blame?

How are you speaking to your partner or children? Do you speak as though they know nothing? Are you patient or do you show a lack of patience when speaking with them?

"There are no beauties in our family. We're just average looking people." I heard this so many times growing up, I grew up believing it, and when I looked at my reflection in the mirror, I saw much less than average. I did not like what I saw reflected back to me. I never saw anything beautiful about me; I could only see what I perceived was ugly. I zeroed in on every single imperfect thing about me. Too skinny, small breasts, crooked smile, thin lips, thin hair, too long of a face: just plain and ugly. My list was long and full of everything I saw wrong in my reflection. My younger sister, who was the rosy-cheeked, blonde beauty in our family, outshone me in my perspective. I spent a great deal of my young adulthood very jealous of her beauty, wishing I could have even a modicum of it.

Feeling unattractive made me feel uncomfortable around others, most of whom I saw as better than me. I was always judging and trying to find anyone who, like me, was ugly or even uglier than me. I was uncomfortable around people, especially attractive ones, because I felt I did not belong. I could not compete, yet that is what us girls were supposed to do: compete for the eyes of men. But I could never be one of the loveable girls and I longed to be seen as worthy of love. Not once did I ever entertain the thought that true, genuine beauty comes from within.

In a patriarchal society, women are raised to believe that their worth depends upon a man. Some religious beliefs even go so far as to say a woman cannot gain her place in heaven without her husband. Why can we not raise our girls to believe in themselves, to believe that their worth lies within themselves, to believe they are deserving of whatever they set their minds to achieve? Through programming and conditioning, it is consistently pushed in front of our girls that beauty is blonde, blue-eyed, pale, white skin, skinny, wearing copious amounts of makeup, skimpy attire, and air-brushed to perfection. If you don't like the way you look, there's Botox, fillers, implants, plastic surgery and many claims of high-priced lotions and serums that will fix your society-dictated deficiencies.

Would it not be far more advantageous to teach our girls not to believe the lies that social media, television programming, and the many beauty magazines constantly feed them? Rather, shouldn't we emphasize that beauty is only skin deep? Let us teach them that true beauty comes from within and that beautiful inside translates to beautiful outside.

I know I was loved by my parents and other family members. I have many, many happy memories of my childhood. As I look back now, I can see how the use of physical punishment, constantly being teased by my dad, and also how being bullied through my school years played a greater role in the shaping of my personality than their love did. It ate away at my self-esteem, transforming me into a woman, who felt little to no respect for myself, no love for myself, and did not deem myself worthy or enough. I would constantly seek validation everywhere to bolster my lack of self-esteem and self-love.

I dimmed my light … I turned it down … I let it burn out.

Constant punishment for transgressions, whether minor or major, damages the delicate psyche of a child who is only just beginning to develop into who they will be.

We are born perfect, but through these various forms of conditioning, our inherent perfection is slowly eroded away, leaving us with a lack of self-love, a lack of confidence in ourselves, a lack of confidence in our abilities, and constantly looking for love and validation outside of ourselves. Our perfection gets pushed down so deep, covered up by the programmed beliefs that we carry, that often as adults, we suffer from mental or emotional illness, even serious physical illnesses.

Everyone makes mistakes, including adults. But as a child, when we are physically punished for them so constantly and consistently that we begin to believe there is something inherently wrong with us. This leads to us carrying guilt and shame throughout our life.

"We don't stop loving the parent who is abusive, but we do stop loving ourselves."

As many of us were told when we show our emotions, which I did aplenty as a child, *"stop that crying, or I'll give you something to really cry about!"* And when little boys display their emotions, they are told, *"boys don't cry," "man up,"* or *"don't be such a Nancy."*

Young girls who are trained to be stoic or keep a stiff upper lip, grow up to be women who have difficulty expressing their emotions. We need to be told that it is okay to take up space, feel our BIG feelings and never, ever hide any part of ourselves. Our little girls need to be told they are indeed as capable as their male counterparts. For a young boy, who throughout his childhood represses his emotions, because boys don't cry, it *will* manifest in anger in adulthood. And raising our children with these very different approaches to showing emotions also sets up our boys to objectify and diminish women.

What does this teach us? We believe if we stop showing our emotions, we will be more lovable. We are striving for the perfection that will make us safe from punishment, and this perfectionism makes us decide, *"if I can't do this perfectly, I won't do it at all."* So, we begin to suppress our emotions, stuffing them down like great wads of cotton until we choke on them. And, we continue pushing them down, hoping they will never surface again.

We learn to be seen and not heard. However, when something or someone triggers us, all those emotions we bottled up and swallowed down can resurface, and we may implode!

The implosion most often shows up as dis-ease, physical suffering, or emotional and mental distress. When we suppress what we should express, it can and will eventually show up. And there are so many ways that it can reveal itself.

As an energy healer, I understand the importance of the *chakras*. There are a total of 144 chakras in the human body, with seven major chakras. The seven major chakras present in the human body are a major center of "prana" energy *(life-energy)*. The seven major chakras, which run from the top of one's head down to the bottom of their spine, are the crown chakra, the third eye chakra, the throat chakra, the heart chakra, the solar plexus chakra, the sacral chakra, and the root chakra. And how do the major chakras affect us? As an example, our throat chakra governs our strength of will, our personal expression, communication, expression, and our ability to speak our truth. When this chakra is balanced, our communication is clear, concise and we are easily able to express our truths.

When we suppress our voice as a child and even as an adult, it closes this chakra, impeding the flow of our life energy, and it shows up physically with chronic sore throat, raspy throat, strep throat, frequent mouth and gum ulcers, laryngitis, swollen glands, and often thyroid problems. I struggled through most of my life with swollen glands and a constant *frog in my throat*. Now, after working to open my throat chakra and speak my truth, I know why. Now that I can speak my truth, the swollen glands, sore throats, and constant frog in my throat have disappeared. My voice is clear. I say what I mean and mean what I say.

If you are struggling with this, see an energy healer—your throat chakra may be closed.

"Maybe it is time for you to speak your truth – *even if your voice shakes*."

Throughout my childhood, I was extremely self-conscious, which left me struggling in the social, competitive, and the occasionally mean atmosphere of traditional schooling. I went through school always believing that everyone was looking at me and judging me for everything that I perceived was wrong with me. I believed that everyone who saw me was thinking the same thing that I was: that they were struck by how ugly I was, how skinny I was, and pitied me as they also knew I would never, ever get a boyfriend. I became the perfect target for the bullies at school, who picked on me for things that were outwardly obvious: my glasses, my thinness, my "funny" shoes. In addition, I was late to develop breasts, thus in my senior years at elementary school, I was teased for not having developed with the other girls.

When I finally got my first bra, which incidentally I really did not need, I frequently found notes on my locker saying, *Barb stuffs her bra*. So many episodes of bullying, which, once again, continued to reinforce that I was not good enough and that I definitely was NOT pretty! The other girls would always poke at me, trying to collapse my bra. Back in the 1960s, bras were stiff and well-padded, so without breasts to fill the cups, when a cup got poked in, it stayed in.

There were so many times I was mortified when someone managed to get a good poke at my bra, leaving me with one cup looking filled out and the other one collapsed. These episodes always ended in explosive laughter at my expense. I was always looking beyond myself for love and validation that I was a good person, that I was pretty and desirable, that I was worthy and capable. That left me in a vulnerable position for those bullies that found great pleasure in picking on people like me— the weak and vulnerable.

In so many ways throughout elementary school, I tried to fit in. I enjoyed learning and studying. I exceled in artistic endeavours and sought to belong by taking part in public speaking competitions, spelling bee competitions, writing, and athletic activities. I did very well in the creative arts, but unfortunately, my undertaking of various athletic endeavours usually ended with me even more hurt and broken. Every sport I attempted was cut short by a different injury. After four separate episodes with broken arms and a broken shoulder, I gave up my dream of becoming an athlete.

It took me so many years to understand that when we bury traumatic events we experience as a child, they go deep down in our body, into the cellular level. As a child, when the flow of energy from a painful event we have experienced is stopped, that event is frozen in our energy field and it remains unhealed at the exact moment in time that it occurred. This creates a block in our energy field, and that part of us remains frozen until we can *metaphorically* thaw it. It does not mature alongside us as our body continues to age. If the event occurred when we were a one-year-old, then that part of our emotional self remains at age one, and it will stay as a one-year-old and behave as a one-year-old would when we are triggered. It will not mature until we allow enough energy to flow into it, which begins the growth process.

Each of us carry within us these energetic blocks that have been frozen in time. We are continually interacting with others from these blocks, interacting with their own blocks. When we are in a difficult situation, in just one moment, you might experience reality with your inner adult, and in the next moment, you could have switched to the side of your wounded child. This is why we experience difficulties in our relationships and communication with others. We are constantly switching from adult consciousness to wounded child consciousness, which occurs when these frozen energetic parts of our psyche are triggered. Often, these frozen childhood energy blocks re-emerge many years later and manifest as an emotional problem.

> **"Repressed traumatic events never go away until we can heal our emotions around them."**

When we are triggered by an event, situation, or person, the inner child who was frozen at the moment of trauma re-emerges, colliding with the adult, setting off an enormous amount of emotional upheaval as we attempt to deal with the current situation. However, the one who is actually dealing with it is the inner child that is still in that frozen space in time. That child is feeling the pain and reliving the trauma that is running on a constant internal movie reel.

As adults, we are often ill-equipped to deal with this ill-tempered child within us, and this is when emotional trauma begins to wreak havoc on our physical bodies. The re-emergence of this buried childhood trauma that has not been healed literally bites us in the proverbial ass, quite often reappearing as physical disease or emotional and mental health issues. If we genuinely wish to heal our childhood traumas, we must embrace our inner child, letting them know we love and forgive them, embracing them as you would any small, hurt child. Only then can we move on and release this pain. We must interrupt the pattern by reframing these traumas in our minds.

As I said earlier, I was not raised in an unhappy home, and I know without a doubt I was deeply loved as a child. However, the constant criticisms wrapped in humour, the severe physical punishments, and my inability to hold onto my sense of self led me down a path to become someone I did not like. The quiet little girl grew into a woman who was always seeking the validation and approval of others, in order to feel any sense of self-worth. I had not yet learned the value of loving myself and seeking my own approval, which is the only opinion and approval that matters.

I allowed self-doubt, self-hatred, and self-judgement to frame who I was. Always placing the bar too high and knowing subconsciously that I couldn't attain it, I consistently sabotaged myself in every effort, every situation, every relationship.

I'll bring this chapter to a close with a strong memory I still have from elementary school, the memory that reminds me of who I was and how I internalized what I felt about myself. I was attending my intermediate school graduation dance. My parents had forbidden me to go, as dancing was not allowed and considered sinful in my family. I lied to them about where I was going that evening and went to the graduation event with a girlfriend. I recall as the celebrations were winding down, they announced the last song would be next. It was a slow song for a "slow dance," Jonathon King's "Everyone's Gone to the Moon."

I'll never forget watching the girls and boys pair up to dance as if they were following an unknown algorithm that I had not been taught. I was left sitting alone on the sidelines, the only girl without a partner. How unloved I felt in that moment, how unworthy, how undeserving.

Exceptional Woman Challenge – MEDITATION

At this point of our journey together, I am challenging you to begin a meditation practice. It is vital that you begin this so you can speak to your inner child, forgive her and re-parent her with all the love and acceptance you can give.

If you have never meditated, you will likely find that the moment you begin, thoughts will begin swirling around in your mind. Do you know that the average person has 6,200 thoughts go through their mind each and every day? And so many of those thoughts are about as valuable as two dogs fighting over a bone, so please do not get discouraged when your squirrel brain takes over. This is normal and why they call it a meditation practice. You must practice it every single day to gain proficiency in it. The goal in meditation is to learn to quiet your mind of all the excessive chatter so you can connect to your Higher Self, God, Divine Source, Creator. You want to be clear so you can hear your inner guidance.

Meditation offers so very many benefits, a few of which are:

- An elevation of our mood,
- Feelings of love for one's self
- Lowered blood pressure
- Better sleep

By searching on the Internet, you can find a plethora of guided meditations either on YouTube or in apps through Apple or Google Play. You can simply start with a relaxation meditation or if you feel ready, choose an inner child meditation.

Begin by closing your eyes and focusing on your breath. If you are uncomfortable closing your eyes, choose an object to gaze at. A candle works great here. Some video-based meditations feature beautiful images of nature that you can watch as you listen. You don't need to do any special deep breathing, simply breathe in and out and pay attention to it. Feel the coolness of air as it flows in through your nostrils, and notice how it has warmed when you breathe out.

If you find yourself thinking about what to make for dinner, simply acknowledge the thought and then release it. Endeavour to keep your mind as clear and empty as you possibly can. Release any thoughts by bringing your attention back to your breath. Be sure to listen for your inner voice and intuitive thoughts that may come.

I would encourage you to meditate for ten days in a row. You don't need much more than five to ten minutes of meditation to begin, and you may naturally feel like spending more time in meditation. Make a record of how you feel when you start your ten days of meditation and after the ten days, check in with your feelings and emotions. If you don't feel or notice any improvements, continue this practice for another ten days.

Chapter Two

Looking for Love in All the Wrong Places

When I graduated elementary school and entered high school, I was overwhelmed by the enormity of the secondary school I was attending. It was a very large institution with so many wings, so many halls, so many classrooms, so many teachers, and so many students. Although the bullying had been unrelenting in elementary school, I missed the small, closer atmosphere, where everyone knew each other.

Education seemed so much more serious here; I felt out-of-place. Small and insignificant. As I wandered from class to class on that first day, a new realization hit me: now I was expected to conform, and perform at a much higher level. Now I was to make large decisions about my life's journey and career, yet it seemed the transition was shockingly sudden. I felt younger than the other girls, and in this new system, it seemed there was no room for fun.

By the second week, still learning the rules and the route from one class to the other, I was anxious yet anonymous in the mass of students but getting used to it. I was race-walking to my English class, terrified of being late, and chewing gum that I had forgotten to spit out. I felt a smack across the back of my head, and I spun around.

"Young lady," said the Vice Principal in a tone I recognized. The bile of fear rose in my chest; my heart pounded as I hugged my books tighter to my chest and immediately shrank in my shoes. I looked up at this mountain of a man. In a booming voice, he asked, "Are you chewing gum?" In my fear, it seemed he was breathing fire as his eyes shot daggers right through me.

I was choking; I could not speak, so I simply nodded my head in submission. The other students around me stopped and stared.

His look of disgust increased. It was almost cartoonish. "Get rid of it NOW, or you will face immediate suspension."

My eyes downcast, I nodded as he then continued his march down the hall. I felt so belittled, so shamed, and once again, so unloved. My father was extremely upset that the VP had smacked me on the back of my head and went to the school, irate. This was the only time in my life I recall my dad standing up for me and my rights.

The only redeeming factor in my first weeks of high school was Ron, my very first crush: a senior and a football player. He never even knew I existed, but in my child's mind, I thoroughly enjoyed the different scenarios I could dream up every time I saw him walking down the hall. He had the most beautiful, piercing blue eyes, light brunette, always disheveled hair, and whenever he passed me in the hallway, my young girl's heart fluttered. If there was a chance connection as our eyes met, I simply melted. In those few seconds, everything else faded away, and it made my time there worth it. However, a few months into ninth grade, not even my infatuation with my imaginary football boyfriend could keep me happy or comfortable, so I constantly created imagined illnesses in order to stay home from school.

I can now see I was suffering from severe anxiety. As an introvert, the tremendous number of students overwhelmed me. At the time, however, my parents only saw me as a rebellious and troublesome teenager. Traditional schooling was not working for me. I was an artistic and creative person. I did not fit the school board's model of an average student, which is what the curriculum was, and still is, written around. The school system does not work for every child, and I was one of those children. For me, it was like trying to fit a puzzle piece where it does not belong.

I continually nagged my parents—day and night—for their permission to quit school, but they would not allow it. Eventually, a couple months into grade nine, seeing my unhappiness and my continued time away from school for illness, they finally gave me permission to leave. However, they said, I had to have some sort of education and skills.

"Acquiring secretarial skills is a wise choice", my parents told me. "With secretarial skills, you can always be a typist or a secretary if you don't find a husband."

I was conditioned to believe this paradigm. It became part of the fabric of my psyche. I truly believed my worth, my value, and my beauty were measured by whether or not I could catch a man.

We investigated a couple of business colleges, and they enrolled me in a private one. I loved attending this small school run by an older lady and her husband. I never met Mr. Weller, but I remember Mrs. Weller vividly. A tall, slender woman, her hair rolled up along the sides and the back into three buns with restrained curls on the top. Her glasses were always down on the bottom of her nose, and if you got the look over those glasses, you knew you would be receiving a speaking to. It was an old, well-established school and run like a well-oiled machine—very strict! The schoolmaster ensured that we young women learned the finer arts of "being a lady." I loved my new, much older, and wiser friends, and especially my new freedom as I had to travel daily into Toronto, "the big city", to attend my classes. Plus, I loved the subjects I studied. I experienced no problems at this new school. I exceled in my studies, particularly in my business courses.

One-and-one-half years later, graduating with a ninety-six percent average, I was hired by a large brokerage firm in downtown Toronto as a receptionist/secretary. It was exciting to begin my working career in Toronto.

I felt very grown up, as I rose each morning to catch the bus that took me from east Scarborough to the subway station at Eglinton & Yonge Street in Toronto. And now I was working for powerful stockbrokers. The bustle of the office, with the market opening each morning and the many trades that happened each and every moment, was intoxicating.

I was seventeen years old and free. I soon found myself in my very first relationship with one of the brokers that I worked for. Bernie was in his late forties and married with children older than I was. His constant interest and kindness towards me overwhelmed me. Remember: I thrived on attention, validation, and compliments.

After a few weeks of small, gentle touches, a hand on my back that stayed a little too long, many visits to chat at my desk or calling me into his office to talk, my handsome, older boss, Bernie, progressed to taking me occasionally out to lunch. One day, he took me to a restaurant in Mississauga near the lake. Following our lovely lunch, he drove down to the lake. Parked in his car—a Jaguar—enjoying the beautiful day and the water, he slowly began to kiss me, progressing very quickly to much more than I was ready for.

He was soothing and gentle with me, acting as if this was what we both wanted. I went along with it and tried to relax. After a little time with foreplay, I watched as he opened a packet he took out of his pocket. It was a blue condom, and I watched as he rolled it on over his penis. My mind went into overdrive. I had not, or my subconscious chose not to let my mind entertain the thought that what I was doing with this man would end up with me in this situation. My many thoughts were running through my mind in slow motion. And as I watched him, I was horrified that he would tear me apart. I had never seen the penis of a full-grown man, only that of my little brother's.

We were in the back seat of his car, and I soon found myself terrified. I was nearly naked, weeping and begging for him to stop.

The assault by someone I had trusted, respected, and looked up to was almost more than I could bear. I wept for my loss of innocence and I wept from my overwhelming guilt and shame. I had lost my virginity. There was a tiny part of me that had enjoyed some parts of this experience, causing my shame and guilt to intensify, but the larger part of me was horrified by what I was allowing myself to be involved in.

I had been taught that sex was only for marriage and that I should never allow a man to touch me unless he was my husband. In fact, my mother once told me that she had never kissed any man except my father, and I knew they did not marry until she was twenty-five years of age. I was overwhelmed by guilt—what if my parents found out what I had done? The religious atmosphere that had conditioned my thought process was a highly judgemental one. Judgement for those who did not adhere to the beliefs we held, judgement for anyone who did something that my parents felt was not in line with our beliefs, judgement even for other religious beliefs.

During my young teenage years, our neighbor's unmarried daughter, Susan, became pregnant. I can remember overhearing my parent's very judgemental conversations about her and the shame her parents had to be feeling. Every conversation centered around their disgust at such a young woman falling pregnant out of wedlock, the shame and embarrassment for her parents, and how she had ruined her life.

Susan disappeared and returned a few months later with no baby and everything was seemingly back to normal. In the sixties, this was how unplanned, unmarried pregnancies were handled—with shame, with shutting down, with hiding it away as if it were a tumour that needed to be cut out, with absolutely no acknowledgement of the creation of a new life, and eventually without a baby. There was even a private home established for unwed mothers in Scarborough, not too far from my home. It was one of those buildings that everyone knew what it was for and who lived there, but no one spoke the words.

All of these overheard conversations, the high levels of judgement, the impossible moral compass had me warring within myself. The young woman that was emerging felt the rush of hormones pushing me into a desire to experiment with sex, but the prudish young girl that had been conditioned to believe it was sinful was always there listening in and screaming, *YOU are a sinner! Filthy girl: you WILL burn in hell for these immoral thoughts.*

I didn't see that all the attention, all the sweet talk, all the small touches and gifts that Bernie had showered me with had actually been grooming me. At the time, I did not consider that I had been sexually assaulted, as Bernie did not complete the act of intercourse. He performed oral sex on me and tried to enter me; however, it wasn't until many years later that I was able to view this event through a different lens which allowed me to understand it as sexual assault. Only with more knowledge could I see that this was truly a sexual assault by a man who had groomed a child to satisfy his sexual appetite. In fact, the law would view this as a criminal offense with a minor child. Following the incident, I was discreetly fired.

As I continued to search for love and validation to fill the emptiness that always gnawed away within me, I was invited to a party and I met a beautiful man, with piercing almost black eyes, a very full and thick head of dark chestnut, wavy hair, standing at 6'1" who paid attention to me. That very first evening, I should have seen the red flags, but the physical attention he showed me, once again, overwhelmed me. I was encouraged to drink *(*another sinful thing to do in accordance with my religious upbringing*)*, and I became inebriated. I don't recall a lot from that evening, as I passed out from the amount of alcohol I had consumed.

I woke up on his bed a few hours later, my clothes dishevelled and twisted. Even today, I have no recollection of what did or did not happen that night and we never discussed it because of my embarrassment over the situation. Upon waking, I immediately felt nausea from the alcohol and spent the next couple of hours vomiting. He was kind enough to drive me home, as the friend who had brought me to the party had left without me. When I got inside, my parents took one look at me and expressed their concern and horror. I was covered in hickeys that they both confused with bruising from an assault. I don't recall how I wiggled my way out of that situation. All I remember was I needed to get horizontal and into my bed badly.

The evening left me nauseated and throwing up for nearly three full days. Having never before indulged in alcohol, it was likely that I was experiencing alcohol poisoning. Once recovered, I decided to get back in touch with this tall, dark, and handsome man. I'm sure it was the excitement of someone who seemed so much more worldly than I was, someone who had his own transportation, someone who lived with his brother in their own home that made him irresistible to me. We dated a very short three months when he said he wanted to marry me. My immature mind thought, "this is what love is", rushing forward in anticipation of a wonderful life, children, and a man who adored me.

I was not yet eighteen and rebelling against my parents. I was rebelling against their very strict, religious rules, which I was expected to follow without question. Before I met my husband and I had begun working, I had a fight with my mom and dad and I told them I was moving out. My mother held up a bobby pin and said, "if you leave this home, this is all you'll leave with!"

At the time, getting married seemed like a good way to get out from under their rule, although I needed their legal permission to do so *(which they gave me)*. Towards the end of our marriage, my husband told me that when we got married, he really didn't love me but figured, what the heck—he had nothing better to do at the time.

I was only seventeen-and-a-half years old, and I went into this relationship still believing the biblical principle that women should be subservient to their husbands, so I ended up in a very controlling marriage with a man who ruled by the principle, *it's my way or the highway*. He would regularly tell me, "If you don't like it, the door swings out".

I'd ended up marrying my father.

My husband had to approve any money I wanted to spend. He would be furious if I spent on something he deemed unnecessary. Because of this control, I became involved with petty shoplifting to satisfy my cravings for more. Somewhere deep down, I felt that more would bring me happiness. It did not.

I had no say in our intimate life; it was always on his terms. "No" was not an acceptable word in our marriage, nor was illness or a "headache." Throughout our marriage and sexual life, I continually allowed him to intimidate me, thereby controlling the how and the when. The abuse continued for our entire marriage, and I can remember being woken many nights from a deep sleep, as he was preparing me for intimacy without my permission.

He teased me relentlessly. We regularly went away on weekends with his three brothers and their wives, and his brothers soon joined in with the teasing. On one particular weekend, I was extremely upset over the constant teasing and begged them to stop. "We do it because we love you!" they replied. I had no answer for that. I thought to myself, why would you express love by being mean to someone—what a strange way to show love.

During the first year of our marriage, my husband was unfaithful to me with my best friend. She came to me and told me about their affair, a secret which I kept for many years, not even telling my husband that I knew. You must remember, it was my belief that you marry for life and a woman is expected to be subservient to her husband. I blamed myself for his adultery—obviously, I was not enough; I was unable to keep my husband happy or satisfied. It was me who had done something wrong, not him. So, for the majority of my marriage, I fulfilled the role of a subservient wife, allowing my husband to dominate me in all areas of our life. His financial withholding, the friends we spent time with, the constant criticism all chipped away at the relationship with my family until it was broken. We also had a very difficult sexual relationship where he often reduced me to tears, so I would submit despite the pain of unwanted intercourse.

I had yet to understand that I alone was in charge of my body. NO-ONE had the right to use it without my consent.

It was not too long into our marriage that my health started spiralling downward, first with chronic bladder problems, then difficulties in carrying pregnancies to term. I lost my first son, who died in-vitro at six months, then I suffered miscarriage after miscarriage until I was finally able to carry to term. My first surviving child—a son—was followed by a daughter three years later. Out of my six pregnancies, I only carried two to term.

The birth of my second (and only surviving) son was difficult. After over thirty hours—with fifteen of them in "hard labour"— my son was born, however, not without intervention. He was extracted with forceps, leaving me with fourth-degree lacerations requiring multiple layers of stitching to close the opening that had torn open between my vagina and rectum from the forceps and a large baby. My doctor later said that I would have had an easier recovery had I undergone a caesarean section. Following the birth, I overheard my husband joking with some friends, saying the birth was great. When he was directly asked how I was, he said, "It was like having a sliver removed." Neither empathy nor compassion were emotions he showed me.

A couple of weeks after the birth of my son, my husband and I were involved in a head-on collision with a drunk driver on our way home from a business meeting. To this day, I thank God that my baby boy was home safe with my mother and not in our car. There were no seat belt laws in the seventies, so I was not belted in, nor would my baby have been. I was curled up asleep in the front seat when the collision occurred. The sound of tires squealing as the cars collided brought me back to consciousness. Metal slamming into metal; its twisting and fracturing is a sound I will never forget. The impact threw me into the windshield, fracturing my skull, then I was thrown backwards and down under the dashboard. I lost consciousness.

I woke up under the dashboard with the engine pushed in over top of me. Both my husband and I wore glasses, which were thrown off in the accident. I distinctly remember both of us fumbling around for our glasses. He grabbed mine, put them on, and screamed, "I can't see. Something has happened to my eyes." This was not funny at the time, but we often had a good chuckle about this many years later.

I sustained a fractured skull requiring stitches to close my head wound, whiplash, and a serious concussion which served to compound my already multiplying physical issues. I found out many years later from MRIs and cat scans for my chronic head pain that I had also sustained two compression fractures in my neck, which were not diagnosed or treated at the time.

I spent a full year in physical rehabilitation with physiotherapists, occupational therapists, and massage therapists for my injuries. During my recovery, I was so grateful for my mother; she spent copious amounts of time with me to help with my son. It was difficult to manage him because of the pain I endured from my injuries. Remember, I had a husband who did not believe, as the man of the house, he should have to do any cooking, cleaning, or taking care of babies. He never once got up for a night feeding or changed a diaper with either of our children.

Looking back now, I believe I would have been diagnosed with postpartum depression. My first babe had terrible colic and cried so very much. He was so difficult to soothe, even rocking him didn't stop the crying. During the night, when he wouldn't settle, I would have him beside me in his bassinet screaming on one side and my husband on the other side yelling at me to shut the baby up, as he had to get up at 5:00 am for work. I cried through the first six months with my boy. I felt so very alone. Had it not been for the kindness of my mother, I don't know how I would have coped.

The birth of my daughter was no less traumatic. During her birth, as she descended through the birth canal, a large, previously undiscovered growth exploded on her head as she made her entrance into the world. She was whisked away to the NICU and I didn't see her for over twenty-four hours. The growth turned out to be benign, so she was eventually brought to me.

However, my girl did not have the easiest start in life. She was born with a blood disorder where her white blood cell count would cyclically drop precariously low, leaving her open to illness after illness. Unfortunately, this disease, cyclic neutropenia, was not diagnosed until she was fifteen years old. She spent her first three months in and out of the hospital with different issues—bacterial infections, inability to keep food down, and more. The list of health problems continued to grow. It was so difficult being separated from my babe, and I can still hear her screams as she endured test after test to determine what was wrong with her.

Her birth left me with a prolapsed uterus. My doctor recommended no more babies due to the difficulties I had experienced in carrying to term. I asked my husband if he would undergo a vasectomy so we would not have to worry about birth control. He absolutely refused, saying, "no one is touching the family jewels."

With everything I had gone through, I had to undergo yet another surgery as I submitted to a tubal ligation to prevent any more pregnancies. Although the possibility of pregnancy was resolved, I continued to experience severe menstrual cycles with heavy, heavy bleeding, often lasting as long as two weeks. This was accompanied by debilitating pain. During my cycle, my blood loss was so heavy that I often became anemic and experienced severe fatigue. Many methods were tried to make my periods more bearable, including using birth control pills, and I underwent four dilation and curettage procedures. At twenty-six years of age, after nine years of failed pregnancy after pregnancy and two difficult births, I followed my doctor's advice, and I underwent a partial hysterectomy.

This surgery was done vaginally. My doctor's instructions were no heavy lifting (nothing heavier than a fork) for eight weeks and to avoid any intimacy for a minimum of eight weeks due to the hundreds of internal stitches required to complete the surgery. Three weeks following this major surgery, my husband, playing on my guilt and my inability to say no, pressured me into sexual intercourse before my recovery period was over.

Within a day, I began experiencing severe abdominal pain and was rushed to the hospital with *cuff cellulitis* (a pelvic infection) that was severe enough to threaten my life. As I lay in the hospital's emergency department in severe pain from this infection, I was immediately put on two different intravenous drips—antibiotics and narcotic pain killers, after which I was sent home.

Within hours, through a morphine-induced haze, I noticed something felt wrong. It started with what appeared to be a prickly, blistery, heat rash, and then over the course of two days, it turned into what looked like a severe sunburn over my entire body. Then my joints began stiffening and swelling, and I was having trouble with my breathing. Rushing back to the hospital, I was told it was an allergic reaction to penicillin and gentamicin, antibiotics I had experienced a mild reaction to years earlier.

When I was admitted to the hospital with my infection, they fitted me with a hospital administered bright red allergy bracelet to highlight my allergies to medication, and I was also wearing my Medic Alert bracelet. Still, the doctor ordered the very antibiotics I had previously experienced *mild* allergic reactions to. This time, however, the reaction was far more severe. This allergic reaction to the antibiotics prolonged my recovery by months. My doctors had to carefully monitor my reaction to antibiotics, and they frequently changed my medication in an effort to get rid of my infection. I left the hospital on oral steroids to continue managing my allergic reaction, which was followed by a full eight months of weaning off the corticosteroids.

Once I did recover, my father pushed me to pursue legal action against the doctor and hospital. This was the first time in my life that I felt some control in forcing the medical establishment to investigate their lack of care, although I found it to be a terribly unpleasant experience. It gave me some satisfaction that there were repercussions for their thoughtless actions that could have cost me my life. I was told I should never ingest penicillin and gentamicin again as I may not be as lucky the next time.

My ob/gyn surgeon, who was named in the suit, was stunned by the lawsuit. He called to interrogate me over the phone, wanting to know why I was doing this to him. I was extremely intimidated by his forceful questioning. "I was faced with giving you the best, strongest, and quickest antibiotics to stop the infection in order to save your life," he insisted as I tried to end the call.

I had no understanding whatsoever of legal dealings and was reprimanded by my lawyer and instructed not to speak to anyone other than him moving forward. I was left out of much of the back-and-forth discussions between lawyers, discoveries, and many offers that were rejected by my lawyer. The lawsuit finally settled after a full year of legal battling; the stress compounded the symptoms of my already overflowing bag of illness and emotional turmoil. The only satisfaction I got out of the whole ordeal was that the doctor was reprimanded for his careless handling of my case, and I received a small settlement for nearly losing my life. At the time, I recall thinking, *was this settlement amount all that my life was worth?*

Exceptional Woman Challenge: LOOK INTO YOUR VALUE

I would like to challenge you to look deeply into your worth, your value. How are you treated in your life by your family and friends? Are you treated with respect, valued as an important, contributing member of society? Or are you abused verbally, physically, emotionally? This won't be an easy challenge, but I encourage you to look closely.

Journaling will help here. The only way you can heal is to face these difficult challenges head-on, digging deep into your thoughts, reactions and emotions, that surround your relationships. Write down everything you feel about these relationships—whatever comes into your mind.

Remember, you ARE worthy, you ARE enough, you ARE deserving.

Chapter Three

The Computer Age

After raising my children to school age, and needing the additional finances to make ends meet, I went back to work as a legal secretary. I was employed as a legal assistant at a well-established law firm in downtown Toronto. I thoroughly enjoyed my job working for one of the senior partners. During my time there, the company decided to move from IBM electric typewriters to Wang OIS stand-alone word processors.

I was totally fascinated by the capability of these marvelous machines. No more typing and retyping an entire page because of one little typo. You could make a mistake, back up, and correct it instantly. What a miraculous invention! I was in love with this new technology, so I decided I would go back to night school at a nearby community college to study computer sciences.

Shortly before I finished my studies, I applied for and obtained a job in the IT world. My position was Computer Software Support Specialist with Wang Canada, supporting the word processing software and systems they created. A whole new, exciting world opened up to me as I discovered a new confidence in myself through this incredible learning experience, which I had never before experienced. I discovered I had a natural aptitude for system software. I made new friends and began to enjoy a life outside of my marriage. I was valued for my contribution in a national support centre for a large computer firm.

As my confidence grew, I could feel the love and respect for my husband slowly crumbling, and I knew separation was inevitable. It was only a matter of time.

I was thirty-one years of age when our marriage of nearly fourteen years came to an end. We made the decision that I would move out and my husband would keep the family home where our children could remain in their familiar surroundings, with their friends and schooling. The separation had come as a huge shock for them, as they had been raised in a peaceful home. There was no fighting. I simply followed what I knew my husband expected of me. The only problem with living this way was that I, the real Barb, was slowly dying. My inner light dimmed and was burning out.

I rented an apartment and left my two children with my husband in the hopes that their lives would not be completely turned upside down while I learned how to be alone for the very first time in my life. When I told my parents of my separation, my father stood up from the table and said, "you know what people will think about a woman who leaves her husband and children," and walked out of the room.

Throughout my life, I have always been very easily influenced by other people's opinions. My husband's constant criticism of my mother and father—how they did or did not parent, along with everything else he perceived as wrong with them—eventually damaged my relationship with my parents, and I saw very little of them during my marriage. My father's reaction pushed me yet further away. Two weeks following my announcement to my mom and dad, my dad called me at work and apologized for what he had said and how he treated me. This was the beginning of the mending of our relationship. Without my ex-husband's interference, I finally grew to enjoy and love time with my parents.

I chose a two-bedroom apartment on the fifth floor of a building in the east end of Toronto. My windows overlooked the lovely gardens and outdoor pool on the building's property. I can still remember the profound loneliness I felt the day I moved into my apartment without my children. I was alone for the very first time in my life. I kept it together and even felt some excitement right up until I closed the door behind the movers. I stood there staring at that door for a few minutes, feeling the weight and the enormity of this choice I had made. I turned around. This was totally foreign to me, a brand-new home by myself, no husband, no children.

I stood there with some of my familiar belongings, the scent of freshly painted walls lingering in the air, and I momentarily felt gratitude for having amicably divided my own belongings from my husband's. Although this wasn't home, there was a modicum of familiarity when I looked at the boxes, my sofa, and some of my other personal belongings. But still, they looked like the possessions of someone else. I had never felt such a profound feeling of loss. The silence in that apartment at that moment was deafening, interrupted only by the low hum of the refrigerator, so I plugged in my television and allowed a gameshow to drown out the silence. Through the un-curtained window, I looked out at the beautiful foliage of the trees on the apartment grounds.

For the first few weeks, I was terrified of the quiet of my apartment. Even being alone in the darkness terrified me. The beige colour of the walls was impersonal and definitely not me. I sat wondering what my children were doing in the house I had decorated and lived in throughout our marriage. I was too scared to sleep in my bedroom, so I had many restless nights on my sofa in the living room with all the lights on and the television going. My husband could see that the loneliness was getting to me and suggested that, although we were living apart, we should maintain our physical relationship.

"If we maintain a physical relationship and you give me what I need, I will not date other women," he said. It may be that I thought maintaining our intimate relationship would absolve me of some of the guilt I felt for leaving the family home. It may have been that his suggestion made it seem that he thought this separation was temporary and that someday I would come back to him, begging to be allowed back in. Regardless of what he did or did not think or his reasonings, I did as he suggested and allowed our physical relationship to continue. I can clearly remember how disgusted it made me feel.

Guilt plagued me. The guilt of breaking up my family, the guilt of continuing to have an intimate relationship with my husband when I knew I had no intention of ever reconciling with this man, the guilt of leaving my children to begin a new life without them.

I started working long hours to cope with the loss of my family. I would go out to bars with work friends, staying out till the wee hours of the morning to keep me from the loneliness I felt when I was home alone in my apartment. I drank far more than I ever had before. There were times when the depression and loneliness were so overwhelming, I seriously thought about taking my life. I had given up smoking many, many years previously but started up again when I was out with friends. I needed to be with friends rather than home alone, where my thoughts would take me to very dark places.

One evening after spending time out with friends, the loneliness of my empty apartment overwhelmed me, and I stood there thinking, *how can I possibly live the rest of my life like this?* I went to my medicine cabinet and picked up a bottle of aspirin, which was all I had at the time. Weeping with loneliness and despair, I fell to the floor, sitting in front of the bathtub, my hand cupped, containing every single tablet that had been in the bottle. How easy it would be to just stop the pain by swallowing a mouthful of them. I could not bear the thought of spending the rest of my life this way. What stopped me from swallowing those pills that night can only be described as

Divine intervention. To this day, I still do not know what stopped me from swallowing that handful of tablets. However, I know now that the Universe had much greater plans for me than I knew or even understood at the time.

When I agreed to maintain a physical relationship with my husband, it never occurred to me to use protection. After all, we were still married. As it turned out, I should have. A few weeks after we resumed our physical relationship, I found myself at my doctor's office requiring antibiotics and creams for a genital virus he had picked up from one of his many relationships.

Six months into my separation, I was missing my children terribly, as well as watching my little girl wilt like a rose; so, at Christmas, I spoke with them about moving in with me. I was beginning to feel better. I was settled into my apartment and my job was going well. I missed my babies and wanted them with me. My daughter was excited to move in with her momma; however, my son wanted to stay with his dad and his friends. So right or wrong, this is what we did. My daughter moved in with me and my son stayed with his dad.

My family was further destroyed. Two new families were created, driving a deep wedge into the relationship between my two children and driving a wedge between me and my son. My daughter and her dad eventually lost their relationship.

It took me many years and many tears, berating myself for what I did or did not do, shaming myself over my poor parenting skills, and the loss of these relationships, among many others, to realize that this was the way it was supposed to be. There were many, many years where my son and I were estranged. Did he still love me? Why did he seem distant and withdrawn, not wanting to have a relationship with me? Had I done something to cause this separation between the two of us? Thoughts like this plagued me constantly. So, I learned to stay out of my mother's heart when I thought of my beautiful boy and listen only to my soul's language of love.

A lack of love for myself throughout my lifetime, as well as not seeing that I needed to heal my life, resulted in me causing pain to those I deeply loved. I have found through complete surrender to our Divine creator that many relationships in my life have either healed or closed, which is exactly the way it is supposed to be. My grown son and I continue to rebuild our relationship, expressing deep love for one another easily now. Our love and respect for each other has healed many, many wounds.

Exceptional Woman Challenge: SURRENDER AND ACCEPTANCE

We're going to go a little deeper here. I challenge you to look at your life through the eyes of surrender and acceptance and record your thoughts in your journal.

When we surrender and accept, we are not settling, but giving our life over to our Creator with the knowledge that your life is perfectly perfect and you are where you are supposed to be right now. It may not be where you'll stay forever, but right now, it is what you need for your evolution and growth.

Once you are able to surrender your life and your will to God, you will find acceptance comes easier. You will know without a shadow of a doubt that everything in your life is always perfectly perfect.

Chapter Four

A Fresh Start

When my daughter moved in with me, I moved from my apartment in east Scarborough to a more spacious apartment in Don Mills, which was much closer to my job. Although I was renting a two-bedroom apartment, she and I shared one bedroom. We shared lots of late-night giggles and plenty of time together as mother and daughter. Having her with me helped so much with the loneliness I had experienced when I first moved out on my own.

Although it was wonderful having my daughter with me, she struggled with leaving the familiarity of her friends and school. She was very shy and had trouble settling into a new school where she knew no one. I'll never forget the kindness of the principal at her school, who came by our home each morning to pick up Sebrina in an effort to help her acclimate to the new school and surroundings. She even allowed her to bring her guinea pig to school one day for show and tell. Her kindness made all the difference in the world, enabling Sebrina to settle into our new life together and make new friends.

I was supported through this time by a few very good friends. In particular, I developed a close friendship with a wonderful man I had worked with. He had been steadfast in his friendship and support of me during my difficult separation, sleeping over on my sofa many a night, so I didn't feel so alone and often times staying up till the early morning hours talking to me on the telephone when I was scared and lonely. My new apartment was in an older building, and there was no air conditioning, so one very hot day, Don surprised me with a window unit he installed in our living room to help cool down the apartment.

He was never a romantic man, however, the love he demonstrated for his family reassured me. He was dedicated, steadfast, and always there in time of need. It was not too long before our friendship blossomed into love. Don had never been married, and becoming involved with a divorced woman and ready-made family was something his parents did not support.

We purchased our first home, proceeded with our wedding, and were married two years following my divorce. In the back of my mind, I always carried the knowledge that his parents had tried to dissuade Don from marrying me, so, when I was in their presence, I always felt discomfort as I knew they had disapproved of our relationship.

Following our marriage, I never experienced loving feelings or inclusion as a family member. My children were always referred to as Barb's children. I struggled with how to behave around them due to their lack of emotion and lack of displayed love. Don is Asian, and their culture is very formal. Never once did I see his parents express love for each other with a touch or a hug. My family was always very expressive with hugs and affection. My mom always gave my dad a hug and kiss before she went out.

For years I worked hard to gain the approval of Don's parents, showering them with gifts such as my own hand painted artwork, crocheted Afghans, and lovely clothing (which they never wore). I spent decades feeling excluded and responsible for what I perceived as a lack of love.

Until my awakening and healing, I held deeply onto this pain. Following my years of study in spirituality and energy, I now know that I have been an empath my entire life, but I did not recognize it as such before my awakening. Thus, I wasted far too many, many years holding onto resentment and anger for the way my children and I were treated by my new extended family.

However, no longer is there room in my life for these emotions—through my healing years, I have released the resentment and deep hurt. I have forgiven them so I can experience peace in my life and with the deep knowing that we are all Divine creatures, all created by one source. I also recognize that we were brought into each other's lives for a reason, and I am always expressing profound gratitude for the many, many lessons laid before me through these relationships. We are intricately intertwined through our energetic signature and souls.

Meanwhile, the relationship between Don and my children blossomed. He never attempted to take the place of my children's dad; he simply became a good friend to both of them. Don and I raised my daughter together. We were married when Sebrina was nine years of age. I am profoundly grateful for Don's steadfastness as her father figure and dad. And Sebrina seldom gave us cause for concern until her mid-teens, and then naturally, when she spread her wings, there were conflicts.

For instance, we allowed her to get her license when she started a part-time job at KFC. As she often worked late hours, it was easier to let her drive herself there and back. On one particular evening, she asked to use the car to go to a friend's home in our local area. A few hours after she left, we got a phone call from her girlfriend who said, in a very small voice, "We've been in a little accident".

As Sebrina had not made the call, I immediately asked, "Is Sebrina okay?"

"Yes, she was." Her friend asked, "Could you come get us?"

When I asked where they were, her girlfriend replied they were three towns east—not where they were supposed to be.

When Don and I arrived on the scene, police lights were flashing everywhere. My brand-new Jetta was in a parking lot, the back end completely crushed in as they had backed into a lamppost. The post appeared to be undamaged and was now standing straight up out of the back windshield. This was definitely not a "little" accident.

I ran to my daughter and asked her if she was hurt anywhere. She indicated no. Anger got the better of me, and although I had never used physical punishment with my children, I slapped her across the face. The policeman who was with us immediately whisked Sebrina into the back of his cruiser. When he got her there, he asked her, "does your mother hit you often?" To which she replied in a meek little voice, "only when I wreck her car!"

Years later, we really have been able to have a good chuckle over this entire situation. After ensuring that Sebrina was in no danger from us, the police officer came to Don and me to explain what had happened. Apparently, one of her friends, a fifteen-year-old boy, had persuaded Sebrina to let him drive the car. He obviously was not licensed but told her that because the parking lot was private property, it was perfectly legal for him to drive. When Sebrina saw the miles they had put on the car, she knew she was in trouble as it was much higher than she had been given permission to drive. The young boy, in his innocence, told them that if they drove the car backwards, it would also reverse the mileage they had put on the odometer (remember the 1980s movie, *Ferris Bueller's Day Off*?) So, that is what he proceeded to do: drive rapidly in reverse, and it was he who had smashed into the light post. The officer told me that had the car reversed just millimetres more, they would have hit the gas tank. To this day, I am deeply grateful for those few millimetres.

Exceptional Woman Challenge: YOU DONE GOOD!

Have you ever written a "you done good" list?

I challenge you to sit down and create one. Write down all the things throughout your life that you've done well, that make you feel proud. When you begin, you may feel there's not much; however, once you get started you might be surprised at all the things that begin to come up for you. Keep it handy and add to it as you remember things in your life.

Chapter Five

Gains & Losses

I worked hard to move ahead in my profession, and within a few years, I was hired as a Support Analyst on a team for a large corporation that was installing one of the first fibre optic networks in Canada. My position came with a large learning curve as I had to become familiar with networks from the planning perspective. It was a wonderful opportunity and my dream job, or so I thought.

On the day of my interview, I was directed to the manager's office. His door was open; he was waiting for me when I was escorted in. He was sitting fully reclined behind his desk, his fingers laced behind his head, his legs and feet crossed up on the top of his desk. On seeing me, he pointed to a chair across from him and said, "Sit."

I was so excited by the possibility of winning this position to be part of that innovative project, so I overlooked his rudeness. I put on my pleasant, confident persona and I nailed that interview. Contrary to how I felt about myself inside, I was able to confidently express myself, and whenever in my life I have truly wanted something, I got it. So, I knew I would get this job, and I did. What a celebration we enjoyed when I arrived home to tell my family of my success.

I was hired into a department of six men, where I was the only woman. Large projects such as the ones we worked on rarely go exactly as planned, and when challenges arose, when things did not run smoothly, or we experienced a failure, the witch hunt would begin. It was clear to me, from the questions that the manager would fire at me, that I would end up the one at fault for each system failure. He seemed to derive great pleasure from regularly bullying and emotionally abusing me. For most of my life, I was easily intimated by men or women like this and always saw it as a flaw in my personality, never once stopping to think or see that this controlling, misogynistic behaviour was NOT normal or acceptable in the men or sometimes even the women, who used it to keep other women and me "in their place."

This man took control of every aspect of my job performance, belittling and shaming me in front of my male colleagues. I did not see his intimidating and controlling behaviour for what it was. His rudeness and anger kept me in a high state of anxiety and nervousness, always anticipating with dread that moment when he would walk into my office.

I stayed employed by this firm for eighteen months, and not once did I ever see him smile or enjoy a laugh with the team. I remember thinking the entire time I was employed there: *Why did I not see or pay attention to the red flags of his behaviour during my interview?*

While working at this firm, I experienced the sudden loss of my beloved Gampie, who, if you remember from my first chapter, I felt closer to than my own father. I deeply loved this man and grew up spending many weekends with him and my grandmother, who I called Nannie. When I was fourteen, they moved to Cape Coral, near Fort Myers, Florida, and my parents gave me permission to fly down on my own at age fifteen and live there with them for six months. A wonderful experience for me at such a young age: it was six months of bliss.

I adored my grandfather and I was completely crushed by his death. It was a beautiful, unusually warm Sunday in April. My parents were spending the weekend with us when we received the phone call from my grandmother saying that Gampie had suffered a massive heart attack. I sat on my front porch steps in a state of shock, questioning whether we had even received the phone call. It was my first experience with the death of loved one, and it rocked me to my core. Looking back now at this moment, I can see that my grandfather's death awakened something in me spiritually, as I began hungering for more depth to my life, more substance, more meaning.

I asked for and was given two weeks off work, and upon returning, they fired me. Losing this job was the best thing that could have happened to me, although at the time I didn't see it this way. I was still grieving and then devastated by the loss of my job, which for reasons I'll discuss later, I desperately needed for my own financial health.

The stress I endured at this job, the loss of my grandfather, followed by my termination, as well as the emotionally difficult breakup of my first marriage took a massive toll on my health, and within a very short time, my life exploded into pain, chronic depression, and disability. The fibromyalgia, which had begun after the car accident fourteen years earlier, exploded into chronic pain like nothing I had ever experienced. But as I was newly married with a new home, mortgage, and other financial obligations, I pushed through the pain and quickly moved from this job to another one, working for the president and vice president of a different firm and also providing administrative support for the sales team.

One of the women on the sales team was a controlling, verbally abusive woman. She regularly undermined, berated, and yelled at me to the point where I would sit at my desk shaking with the overflow of strong emotions that I felt but did not know how to process or release. She reduced me to tears more times than I could count. I stayed in this position for only one year, seeking out other employment to get me out of this toxic environment and from under the control of this woman.

Now that I have come through so much healing in my life, I can see all of these controlling situations as nothing more than a continuation of the bullying I experienced as a child. Having not healed my wounds, these people were attracted to my weaknesses like fruit flies to honey. Bullies never bully the strong ones, only the weak ones, that they know they can gain power over.

I now know that these circumstances were introduced into my life for a far greater purpose —the evolution and growth of my soul.

Very shortly afterwards, I found employment with a large multi-national pharmaceutical firm as a software support analyst, running a help desk for their various locations across Canada. This position provided me the opportunity to work both online, over the phone, and on-site with the employees of this firm. I was frontline support, so if I could not resolve the software or hardware issue, I would escalate it to someone who could. I loved the interaction with my users and being of service, which later in the book, you will see is my passion and my purpose. In that position, I worked with a wonderful team, some of whom have remained close friends to this day.

However, it wasn't long before the pain, the fatigue, the chronic depression became more than I could bear. Very rapidly, I became a shadow of my former self and I would occasionally fall asleep at my desk during quiet moments. My inability to cope with even simple daily chores escalated.

Through these years of learning to live with the incessant pain, my children continued to grow, and my daughter was dating a wonderful young man, and soon, we were blessed with the announcement that our first grandchild was on the way! Hearing this news brought me so much joy I almost forgot the pain I was living with on a daily basis.

Let the planning begin, I thought, as I started dreaming and creating for my first grandchild. She and Mike decided to get married; however, my daughter is not a flashy girl, so she wanted only wanted a civil ceremony and a small catered reception in our back garden. One week before the wedding date, she began experiencing low abdominal distress and was rushed to the hospital. She called me so distraught I could barely understand her on the phone, but I did hear and understand her four words, "my baby is dead."

I rushed to the hospital, and at the same time, Mike, too, was moving mountains to get to Markham from downtown Toronto to be with her. I was sitting trying to console her when Mike arrived and ran to us. He wrapped her up in his arms and they cried together. I saw what a compassionate and tremendous young man he was. He displayed such tenderness, and it was obvious how he loved my girl. We were told later that the child she had lost was their first daughter.

We offered to cancel the wedding, to give them time to grieve the loss of their daughter. However, Sebrina wanted to go on with it despite her emotional pain. She felt it would be good to stay busy with the planning. So, on a beautiful day in June, my girl and Michael were married, and Momma was right all those years ago—even almost twenty-five years later, Mike still treats my girl like his bride.

Exceptional Woman Challenge: BE IN CONTROL OF YOUR DASH

Who controls your life? Do you? Is your life controlled by someone you live with or love? Are you surrendered to your Higher Power, with the full knowing that, yes, you are in control and that there is a Divine plan in place from the day you are born until the day you die? Your birth date and your death date are written in stone, but the time between is yours.

One day on your gravestone, it will show your date of birth and your date of death separated by a dash. What are you doing with your "dash"?

I challenge you to look at your life and examine who exactly is holding the strings. Look for nuances in your relationships that may demonstrate you may not be in control of your life. Examine your relationships with your loved ones and your friends as well.

- Are you a people pleaser?
- Do you have trouble saying no?

These are signs that you are NOT the one managing your life. What are you going to do to ensure you are in full control of your life?

Chapter Six

Pain and Deception

As Sebrina's family grew, so did my disabilities. I found myself unable to truly enjoy time with my beautiful grandchildren due to the depression, the pain from fibromyalgia, inflammatory osteoarthritis, atypical trigeminal neuralgia, as well as the overwhelming fatigue.

During the five years I was employed in my position as a help desk support analyst, I underwent four major abdominal surgeries. First, I was rushed in for surgery due to excruciating pain caused by growths on one of my ovaries. After the surgery, I was told that it had not been growths at all, but rather a hydrosalpinx, a fallopian tube that had filled with fluid. The usual treatment for a hydrosalpinx is surgery to remove the tube as it does not normally self-resolve.

One year later, I was experiencing the same intense abdominal pain again. After an ultrasound examination, it was discovered there were, indeed, growths on my ovary. I was rushed into surgery again, but thankfully, after a biopsy, we were told the growths were benign, not cancerous, cystic growths. I remember asking my doctor if he thought he should take both ovaries, but he said, *"no the second one will likely be fine."* Unfortunately, this surgery was quickly followed by growths on my remaining ovary. As they grew in size quickly, this led to a third rushed surgery, and this time, they removed my second fallopian tube and ovary. Once again, the growths which he had been so concerned about turned out to be cyclical ovarian cysts. Without ovaries, I was thrown into menopause in my early forties.

Then one year following these surgeries, I began struggling with urinary incontinence so great that it affected my ability to leave the house. I had washrooms mapped out in plazas, malls, and grocery stations along the route to my destinations. I always knew just how long it would take me to get from our home to the office and that the reality of rush hour traffic delays made the homeward journey even longer. I also began experiencing pain when my husband and I were intimate. After a visit to my doctor and following examination, he informed me that my bladder had partially descended into my vagina and required surgery to lift it back into place. Following this surgery which I was told would be done laparoscopically, I awoke to a surgical incision from hip to hip.

A couple of days after surgery, the catheter was removed. Following the removal of the catheter, one full day passed before I was able to pass urine. Enduring the pain of constantly filling with urine that I could not release was excruciating. As I was still on intravenous fluids, the pain was increasing exponentially each hour as my bladder continued to fill and I was unable to void. This pain, however, was nothing compared to the pain that was triggered when a nurse tried to re-insert the catheter twelve hours later. The pain was so excruciating that I passed out.

After it was back in place, I remember the nurse chuckling saying, "the doctor has you sewn up so tight, you're like a brand new, young virgin. Honey, your husband will be thrilled." This was when I found out that not only had he gone through my abdomen for the repair, but he had also made many, many incisions vaginally to complete it. A couple of years following this surgery, it became necessary for me to undergo reconstructive surgery to repair the damage this doctor had done to my vaginal canal.

Following my surgery, I sustained bladder infection after bladder infection. Unable to diagnose any physical problems for the constant infections, my surgeon kept me on an antibiotic for nearly two full years to combat the infections. This, of course, damaged my already compromised digestive system, killing off whatever good bacteria I had. So then began the uphill battle of suffering from a severe candida infestation, and leaky gut, along with my already diagnosed IBS. In addition, I suffered from unrelenting vaginal yeast infections. I was living on antibiotics while constantly having to offset the effects of them by using fungal medication to control the overgrowth of yeast from this steady diet of antibiotics.

One day while I was sitting in my surgeon's office awaiting my appointment, a gentleman came into the office and served him with legal papers. I was surprised but did not spend too much time thinking about this incident. Shortly after this, I called in once again with bladder infection symptoms. He had his secretary inform me that he no longer felt he could help me and referred me back to my family doctor.

Shortly after that incident, I was contacted by a lawyer who had initiated a class action lawsuit against this doctor. There were nearly five hundred women in this suit. The doctor was being sued for unnecessary surgeries, incorrect diagnoses, and loss of life. My surgeries at his hands were all deemed unnecessary and it was determined that my medical problems could have been resolved in a far less invasive way. I received a small settlement; however, no amount of money could reverse the damage I had suffered at his hands. To this day, I still suffer from major, unexplained, painful complications with my bladder and an excruciatingly painful, autoimmune skin condition in my genital area, which has destroyed any joy of intimacy that my husband and I previously shared. Had I known at the time what was in store for my future, what this doctor took away from me, I would not have settled so quickly. The physical and emotional repercussions from what he did to me and what I've lost will stay with me for the rest of my life.

I continued working at my job through this time of extreme health difficulties. The human resources department worked with me to decrease my workload, to make my workspace more efficient, and to allow me to drop my work week from five to four days to see if it would help with my health issues. This seemed to offer a modicum of relief; however, identifying myself with my illness was so deeply rooted in my psyche that even decreasing my working hours made very little difference in my chronic pain and fatigue.

It was not too long until this working arrangement ceased to work for the firm. They began to push me into coming back to working five days a week and a regular nine-to-five day rather than the flex hours I had enjoyed. The flexibility of my schedule made it possible for me to slip away from my desk at lunch time to visit a nearby chronic pain clinic where I was injected with narcotic pain killers enabling me to continue working through the remainder of my day. The injections calmed the pain for a few hours, but there was nothing I could do to manage the brain fog from taking over one dozen prescriptions for pain, inflammation, sleep disorders and depression. By now, I was in my mid 40's, and required aids to help with my mobility, along with the regular narcotic injections to cope with the chronic pain.

I applied for disability and was qualified to receive a few months of short-term disability; however, surprisingly, I was denied long-term support.

Looking back now, I can see the great many mistakes I made when transitioning from a working employee to a disabled person. Prior to actually making this official, and having always been a conscientious employee, I told my manager that I could no longer manage to work full-time but informed him I would stay for two weeks so he could find my replacement before I applied for long term disability. In hindsight, this was a monumental mistake. It opened the door for the fight that was to ensue with the insurance company. The manager that had seemed so understanding of my health issues was very open with human resources about what I was doing.

They held my two-week notice against me. The insurance company and HR decided that since I could stay on and work for two weeks while they looked for a replacement, I certainly was capable of continuing to work full time. Therefore, I was deemed ineligible for long-term disability.

Over the next few months, I was constantly contacted by human resources by phone calls, letters, and emails asking when I would be returning to full-time work. I got calls from my manager inquiring about my return. With each communication, they threatened the loss of my job if I did not resume my duties, which included a return to five full days and no more flexible hours.

One day they called me into the office for a meeting. I ran into Andrew, my director, in the cafeteria. He seemed surprised and asked me what I was doing there. When I got to human resources, there he was, sitting in the office with the human resources manager. So, his deception reinforced to me just how manipulative and deceitful he had been in this whole situation. I was crushed by his betrayal as we had enjoyed many, many conversations about his own wife, who suffered from RA and lupus, so he had always appeared to show great compassion and empathy towards me and my illnesses. My director, whom I had respected and truly looked up to, had behind my back sabotaged all my efforts to continue working even through all the pain I suffered. To my face, he was always understanding, but when push came to shove, he drove the knife in deep.

During this meeting, I was presented with a package in return for my termination. This termination was a blessing in disguise at the time, but once again, I did not see this. Following my layoff, I called my rheumatologist to sit with her to fill out the long-term disability forms.

I remember while she filled out the forms for my claim, she said to me, "Barb, I can't tell you what to do, but let me say, even if you win—you will lose".

At the time, her words didn't make a lot of sense to me. But when the insurance company denied my claim and I chose to fight their decision, I fully understood her words. Over the next couple of years, I worked with a lawyer to fight my insurance company's decision. For eighteen months, I was followed by insurance investigators on shopping excursions, family outings, medical appointments, even into my church, where their notes stated, "client was able to stand up and sit down three times to sing."

Their intrusion into every aspect of my life, both private and social, left me broken. The problem with their discoveries report was that they only saw me at my best. When I had the rare good day, I ventured out, knowing that I would be able to perform a few errands. They did not follow, photograph, or videotape me in my home on the days when the pain was so overwhelming that I could do nothing but sit and cry. There were no photographs of me when the depression and fatigue were so great that I could barely crawl out of my bed. They were unable to see me on the days when, as I laid on my sofa, I would count the number of steps I would have to take to get to the bathroom or kitchen from where I was. I would lay there agonizing over how many steps I had to take—first to get to the kitchen, then counting how many steps around the kitchen to prepare a meal.

After the discoveries were presented, I ended up dropping the case and settling in order to put the lawsuit behind me. I received a top-up of my lost wages for two years. But the scars were deep, the damage had been done, and yet another traumatic event was added to my ever-growing mountain of issues that later in my life I would have to forgive, accept, and release.

Exceptional Woman Challenge: FORGIVENESS

There is a quote that says, "Forgiveness is not for them, it's for you." Do you struggle with health issues, either physical or mental? Each morning when you rise, look in the mirror and say, "I am in my best possible health today!" Every cell in your body is listening to your every thought and word that you think and speak. So why not think and speak words of love, positivity and gratitude. Reframe your day: you are a survivor, not a victim of your illness.

The Persian poet Sa'di wrote, "I cried because I had no shoes until I saw a man who had no feet." I love this quote as it reminds me, that there is always someone worse off than me and to be grateful for the health I do enjoy.

Are you holding onto resentment or anger from past situations and relationships? I challenge you to take a deep look; pick one relationship or situation that you are struggling with. Whether the person is alive or passed on, I encourage you to sit down and write a letter to this person. Tell them everything: how you feel, how what happened made you feel, how they made you feel. If they have passed on, maybe take your letter to where they are buried (if possible) and read it aloud to them. If not and you do not wish to share it with them, find a trusted friend and share it with them as a proxy. It really helps to get this all off your mind. Then have a burning ceremony, where you take the letter and burn it, thereby releasing the hold that it has over you. As it is burning, repeat the affirmation, "I release my anger and resentment and forgive you." Use the name of the person you are forgiving to increase the power of the affirmation.

Chapter Seven:

Secrets and Lies

My body continued on its path of autoimmune after autoimmune disease ravaging my health. I was diagnosed with fibromyalgia, osteoarthritis, rheumatoid arthritis, atypical trigeminal neuralgia, gastric reflux, hiatus hernia, asthma, eczema, lichen sclerosis, pre-diabetes, severe iron deficiency, high cholesterol, chronic depression, and sleep disorders due to the pain. Most nights I struggled to sleep as I had severe restless leg syndrome that affected not only my legs but my entire body, causing dreadful, uncontrollable agitation.

During this time, I continued seeing the specialist at a pain clinic where I regularly received trigger point injections with a local anesthetic to numb my pain. These sessions were exquisitely painful, but I did gain a modicum of relief that would last for a few weeks. After a few years of doing this and attending the pain clinic regularly for pain injections, I asked my family doctor to allow me to inject painkillers myself. I was trained in administering intramuscular injections by a public health nurse and began self-injecting narcotic pain medication to manage my pain.

When I looked ahead at my future, it did not look joyful. I slowly started investigating, researching, and reading everything I could lay my hands on about my emotional and physical healing. *The Four Agreements*, all the writings by Dr. Wayne Dyer and Louise Hay, *The Secret, The Power of Now, The New Earth, Radical Forgiveness*. The pile of self-help books grew taller and taller and the number of books on my list continued to grow.

And, although I read voraciously and absorbed what I read, something was preventing me from actually putting my new learning into practice. Deep at the root of my health problems, there was that little issue of payoff. What was the payoff that I received from remaining ill? At that point in time, I certainly could not identify what it was, but now, looking back, I can see that whenever I spoke of my disease and suffering, naturally, I received sympathy, which only served to strengthen and build my need to remain in my victim mentality. I received love and compassion, which gave me the validation I needed to feel wanted and loved. My parents treated me like a china doll, just as Gampie used to. I craved that love and the feeling of being so special to them. My illness brought us so much closer together, something that today, now that they are both passed on, I am so grateful for as I remember them with deep and abiding love.

My weight was now in the obese category at over 230 pounds. I dimmed my light and continued to cover up my beautiful authentic self with layer after protective layer of fat. By this point, I was struggling to even move without the use of occasional aids. In addition, it became nearly impossible for me to leave my home due to the constant and urgent digestive distress from IBS that I suffered, combined with the urinary incontinence from the abdominal surgeries. I never knew when it would hit me, so it became necessary for me to stay close to my home in case of emergency. Following the many years of using narcotic pain relievers and three full years on antibiotics, my gut health was destroyed. As seventy percent of our immune system resides in our gut, it was no wonder I was suffering from so many autoimmune diseases. Thus, I seldom left my home. I found myself in bed most days, only venturing out to grocery shop when I was able, or to attend my numerous doctor's appointments.

There was, however, a war raging within me. From the outside, I looked healthy. Many of the autoimmune diseases I suffered from were an internal war my body was constantly fighting, not affecting how I looked on the outside. I had become exceptionally masterful at covering up my pain and my depression by only venturing out when I was having a good day. I was too embarrassed to ask for help, embarrassed to appear anything other than healthy, embarrassed to show any weakness or disability, and yet I fed on the sympathy and attention it brought me. I felt special when I was identified by all my diseases. I was turning into a person even I didn't like. Friends and family did not want to visit with me because of my angry and miserable demeanour. One thought consumed me, "why had life given me the short end of the stick? Why me?" Depression became my comfort, wrapped around me like a thick comforter.

Looking back now, I know I was very fortunate to have met and married my wonderful husband. He married a relatively healthy woman, and as my health declined, he never wavered in his support of me. He stuck by my side through all the difficulties, all the illness, all the surgeries, and the emotional ups and downs in my life. He worked hard to pay off our mortgage, so when I finally left work and was supported by government disability payments, we were mortgage free which certainly provided us with financial breathing room.

Unfortunately, throughout my years of working at the corporate level, I had allowed myself to get caught up in spending exorbitant amounts of money to stay up to date with expensive clothing and impeccably tailored suits that I felt suited my positions. I allowed myself to get into serious personal credit card debt, which I had kept hidden from my husband for years. I was so deep in credit card debt that with my disability payments, I could only make minimum payments on each of my credit cards. With the extremely high interest rates and only making minimum payments, I knew I would never get out of debt. This weighed heavily on me as well as maintaining my secret addiction: spending money. It was an addiction that enabled me to feel better about myself.

Spending was the result of covering up my guilt and shame for my entire life. It fed my sense of worthlessness, my sense of not being enough, my lack of love for myself. Covered in expensive clothing, beautiful jewelry, shoes, boots, and coats made me feel more powerful, more confident. No one could see the real me beneath my expensive wardrobe. I dimmed my light, and my self-worth was low; I hid my hatred of myself by presenting a confident image to the world, an image of a woman who had the world by the tail. I could not see how truly exceptional I was, as my self-hatred was so intense.

Suddenly finding myself out of work and without a regular paycheque coming in, I began to buckle under the tremendous pressure of this debt. My daughter, who had just had her first son, also needed an extra paycheque in their young household, so she and I decided to do daycare from my home. The money we brought in helped with my debt. But with all my health issues, it was tremendously difficult and stressful to oversee the care of six children, all under the age of twelve. It was during this time that I applied for and was approved for Canadian government disability pension, which took off some of the pressure. We decided to stop doing the daycare as it was having a deleterious effect on my health. I also knew in my heart of hearts that I would have to open up and disclose to my husband the large credit card debt I was carrying.

Exceptional Woman Challenge: SELF CARE & SELF LOVE

When we do not feel love for ourselves, and by love, I mean all inclusive, unconditional love for ourselves, we will find comfort in filling that need with something else. It may be compulsive, excessive spending, alcohol or substance abuse, sex addiction. There are so many things that we might turn to in order to fulfill that need.

Let's talk a little about self-care. When you spend time filling your own cup, it becomes somewhat easier to feel love or, at the very least, like for yourself. Here are a few ideas in this challenge to begin a self-care routine for yourself.

- Go to bed a wee bit earlier at night
- Cook yourself a beautiful home cooked meal, light the candles and use the good china
- Move your body for five minutes every single day
- Buy yourself a beautiful journal and write in it every day
- Spend some time each day in nature allowing the sun to penetrate your naked skin (for no more than ten to fifteen minutes in the early morning sun)
- Connect with someone you love

I challenge you to incorporate one or more of these into your life each day. It won't be long before they become a habit, and you will also find that when you are nurturing yourself, your feelings for you will also develop.

Remember, self-care is not optional!

Chapter Eight

Finding my Health Again

As I moved into my fifties, I grew tired and frustrated from conventional medicine telling me the best I could hope for in my lifetime was only to chemically manage the autoimmune diseases I suffered with. Continuing to exist in a drug-induced fog, taking prescription after prescription that did nothing but numb the pain, not to mention my life, was not how I wanted to live. Surely, I thought, there must be a better way to handle my health. So, I started to investigate various modalities of alternative medicine. I made an appointment with a wonderful and helpful naturopathic doctor. I found myself sitting in her office one day hearing the words, "If you don't make some very drastic changes, you will be a very sick woman by the time you are 60." These words turned my world upside down.

> **"A healthy body is built or destroyed one decision at a time."** – Tosca Reno

Frightened for what lay ahead of me with my health spiralling downward, I left the naturopath's office that day and I found myself in a bookstore perusing the food and lifestyle books. One book stood out: Tosca Reno's *The Eat Clean Diet*. Once home, I dove into it, devouring each and every word, and slowly I began incorporating her principles and recipes for clean eating into my life. I gave up dairy, I cut out white flours, white sugars, white pasta, and white rice. Tosca wrote, "Remember, a healthy body is built or destroyed one decision at a time. It's up to you." Her words hit me hard as I realized it truly was up to me. I had allowed my illness and my lifetime conditioning to create a person and a life I did not like, a life I did not want to live and a body I hated, because in my mind, it had turned against me.

As I slowly worked my way through her book, I learned to juice and make green smoothies. I became the green smoothie queen, creating different variations every morning, filling them with different supplements to improve my health while experimenting with all types of greens! My diet consisted of approximately eighty percent vegetables and fruit, and over the next eighteen months, I shed fifty pounds. I continued eating this way and began incorporating a little movement into my days with Nordic walking.

Then, very slowly on my own, I made the decision to begin weaning my body off two anti-depressants, disease suppressants for rheumatoid arthritis, acid blockers for gastroesophageal reflux disease, irritable bowel syndrome and a hiatal hernia, anti-inflammatories for degenerative arthritis, muscle relaxants for fibromyalgia, steroid and rescue inhalers for asthma, anti-convulsant for trigeminal neuralgia, Parkinson's medication for severe restless leg, and my regular narcotic injections for pain management. One dozen prescriptions in total. This was a full two-year journey. There was excruciating pain as my body adjusted to a life without chemicals, but eventually I was able to release every single one of those prescriptions and today I continue to manage my health with a clean diet, supplementation, and a radically reframed mindset.

Feeling clean and clear, I thought, *"Life is good!"* But as I would soon discover, the Universe was not quite done with me. There was still more work to be done to prepare me for the growth I was about to experience.

I had believed that healing my body was the end of it, never once contemplating or, at this point in my journey, understanding that my emotional and spiritual health, or lack thereof, was what had brought me to this place of physical illness in the first place. I was soon to be faced with a new journey that tore my emotional health to shreds, forcing me to rebuild everything from the bottom up.

I would create an exceptional life and come to fall in love with my flawsomeness, but first, there was to be emotional pain—pain like I had never before experienced, pain that would bring me to my knees. However, the pain was necessary for me to be crushed and despairing. And in my despair, when my ground was tilled and softened, the seeds that I had previously planted began to grow. I would finally begin the journey to re-mold myself into the woman I was meant to be.

That exceptional version of me that had been patiently waiting in the shadows for an opportunity to emerge all along.

Exceptional Woman Challenge: FROM LACK TO ABUNDANCE

I challenge you here to look deeply into your thought process around abundance or lack. Are you always wishing for more, or are you grateful for what you already have? Do you look at your money situation and constantly complain you are broke? Are you grateful that you are able to put a roof over your head and food on your table? Do you suffer from chronic pain or illness?

It is vital that you change your perspective from one of lack to one of abundance.

Begin to give gratitude daily for what you already have. If you suffer from chronic illness or pain as I did, I challenge you to radically reframe your mindset. When you rise every morning, start your day with this affirmation, "I am in my best possible health today". Every cell in your body is listening to your every thought and by simply changing to a positive affirmation *(you are not saying you're not ill, simply reframing it with a more positive spin)*, you will soon find that you see yourself and your illnesses, traumas, and/or losses in a different light.

Chapter Nine

Profound Loss

I began a new and unknown journey into a heart and soul-crushing loss over the next few years. It began with the devastating news that my eldest sister, Gina, was diagnosed with AML (acute myelogenous leukemia), and although she heroically battled for eighteen months, she ultimately lost her battle at sixty-four years young.

Through the months of her illness, we spent a great deal of time together, for which I am profoundly grateful, snatching a few days here and there between her treatments at Toronto's Princess Margaret Hospital. She would often come to my home and stay with me, where we enjoyed many tea parties, late-night chats, and time just loving each other deeply. I grew to know and love this sister I had grown up without, as she had married and left home when I was only three years old, immediately beginning her family. The age difference of fifteen years between us kept me from really getting to know her. I was so grateful for the short time we had together to rediscover each other and share a deep and abiding love before her death. And on my pinky finger I still wear the tiny, gold ring that she gave me at three years of age for being the flower girl at her wedding. It has been sized and rebuilt so many times. The engraved "B" has long since gone, but I cherish that ring and the memory it holds for me of my precious sister.

I still chuckle when I think of the many times we sat up laughing till the wee hours of the morning. Gina was a very stylish woman and never wanted anyone to see her without her makeup or her wigs after she lost her hair. On one particular evening, I came downstairs after getting ready for bed and was startled to see, sitting on my sofa, what I thought was an animal. Turned out it was her wig! When Gina took it off and put it on the sofa, it stayed in the exact shape it had been while on her head, full and round. She knew I would laugh at the wig, so she left it there for me. We both collapsed in laughter, and after that day, she never minded me seeing her natural beauty, with or without her wigs.

Gina's death was followed two years later by the passing of my father. He died after suffering for weeks with spasms in his esophagus, preventing him from keeping any food or nourishment in his body. For weeks, we sat helplessly watching him slowly starve to death. He was kept on IV fluids until his veins collapsed, at which point there was nothing more they could do. I am so grateful, though, for those last weeks with him and my mom. I shared more love in those three short weeks with my dad than I had felt in my entire life. It was a beautiful, healing time for me. I held his hand, and as he took his final breaths. I was able to let him go, knowing he truly loved me. Throughout my father's illness, I spent time journaling, preserving my memories on paper, so I would always remember the time we spent together. These are my unedited feelings from the last few days with my father.

> *"It is nearly midnight and my thoughts constantly drift to my father. I feel I must write to ensure that some of my feelings and thoughts from these days are never forgotten, but engraved in my memory to draw strength from in the days and weeks to come.*

Seeing the futility in my mom's face this week as she nurses my dad, doing everything in her power to prevent the inevitable outcome of this health crisis, has been almost more than I can bear and then to ponder the fact that all this pain she feels right now will not subside but will explode into the depths of grief when the time comes. They have been together 59 years—a lifetime.

Through all the tears, a beautiful door has opened to me as I spend each day with my mom and dad.

Talking with my dad about his death, for which he is prepared and waiting for. Dad has a very deep faith in God and looks forward to the freeing of his soul from his body which is wracked with pain, and then being re-united in heaven with his Saviour. Yesterday as we shared, he likened his life's energy to the falling autumn leaves on a tree. We spoke of love, life, and death, we shared our love for each other.

I fed him this week. I held his hand and just sat with him quietly when no words were necessary. All past wounds are healed … forgotten … forgiven.

As I reflect on these past few days, when the time comes that he will leave his earthly body, I will be comforted by the fact that my father loved me and oh how I loved him.

Today I sat on his bed and held him in my arms like I would hold one of my grandbabies while my mother fed him. He sat up—me behind, him in front with my arms around him so he would not fall, and as he laid his head against my cheek, I felt the tears silently slip from my eyes for the father I knew I may soon lose, whether from this health crisis or if we are fortunate enough to pull him through this, in the not-too-distant future. This is an incredibly hard journey, sitting hour after hour, slowly watching my father die.

I feel strong, then weak. I feel love, then hate. I feel compassion, then anger. I feel frustration, then acceptance. I feel restlessness, then peace. I am awash with so many emotions that tonight sleep eludes me.

In the earlier days of my father's illness, we were able to sit and talk. Now I just sit and watch as he grows weaker and weaker, slipping in and out of consciousness. When he wakes, he suffers pain, restlessness, dehydration & discomfort.

But then through this emotional warfare, I see that this is his final gift to me as I care for him during his last days. Yesterday when he was slightly more lucid, I sat beside him as he slept. He woke and asked me what I was doing there. I replied, "just sitting with you to keep you company". I told him I loved him and he replied that he loved me too, then smiled and drifted back to sleep. A very small moment but a memory that I will cherish.

Today my daughter came to visit her poppa. When she embraced him, his tears flowed with the love he felt for my child, another memory I will cherish. How many more moments will he have that I can collect memories from to hold in my heart for a lifetime?

Each time I say goodbye, is it the last goodbye? When I left tonight, I stole into his room to give him a kiss goodnight and tell him once again how much I loved him, but he slept. He did not know I was there as I stroked his cheek and felt the newly grown whiskers on his face. The softness of his whiskers against my face must be lovingly recorded and filed away with all my other cherished memories. As I left, I touched my fingers to my lips to press a kiss on his forehead, and I wonder, will tonight be the night that I lose my dad. Will that be the last kiss I ever give him?

Since Wednesday, he has slipped further and further away from us. Today he asked mom three times to send me down to see him. When

I got to his room and asked him what he wanted, he said, "I just wanted to see you."

The cycle of life has come full circle. My father is like an infant, unable to perform anything in caring for himself. The simple acts of washing himself, brushing his teeth, putting on a pair of socks, even urinating have all dropped away like the last leaves before the cold breath of winter. What must this be like for a man who was once dignified, modest and proud?

Why should a man who devoted his life to God suffer like this? I am angry that he must end his life in suffering. This journey our spirit must make as we cross from this life to the next should not start like this. Why, why, why? Writer Charles Spurgeon, known as the "Prince of Preachers" in reformed Baptist circles and whose work my father cherished, once said, "death is but the birth pains to a new life".

Dad has always been outspoken in his life, never shrinking from a challenge ... but this challenge to his very life is a war he cannot win. "Oh death - where is thy victory, oh grave where is thy sting". As I sit and witness this slow deterioration, I pray night after night that he will be released from his suffering.

One day after I wrote this last entry, my father peacefully passed away, with my mother, my brother, my daughter, my husband, and me by his side.

Four short years later *(almost to the exact day)*, my mother passed away. There still are no words to describe the loss that I felt at having her ripped from my life. I had been her primary caregiver for six years—helping her and my dad before his death with all their banking/financial needs, shopping, attending to all their medical appointments, ensuring medications were properly counted and in my mom's final years arranging for her pharmacy to use convenience packs and deliver her medications to her door. I was her liaison to the outside world. If there was a medical emergency, I was there day or night. I spent one, sometimes two days every week with her, enjoying shopping or just visiting and then lunch at the retirement home where she lived. I even got to know her friends and enjoyed their company too.

For months prior to her death, my mother had been trying to manage pain in her thighs which brought on severe muscle spasms every minute or so. On this particular night, it was too much for her; she could not bear it any longer, so I brought her to the hospital where we waited almost eight hours in emergency and got no real answers. *(I have since researched and discovered that the pain she was experiencing was muscle breakdown and is a side effect of the statins that most doctors prescribe for high cholesterol. She had been prescribed statins and took them for over two decades).* Instead, she was discharged with a prescription for a strong narcotic. I recall questioning the doctor on call if he thought she would she be alright to go home, where she lived alone, on such a strong drug. She had already been given quite a lot at the hospital and was in and out of consciousness from it. He reassured me that she would be fine and signed the discharge.

I took her home to her cozy apartment in the retirement home and stayed with her until the following night when I was so exhausted that I had to go to my own home for some sleep. We decided I would stay until her bedtime, get her comfortable, before leaving. I helped her to put on a pair of disposable incontinence underpants and we agreed she would not get out of bed until I returned in the morning. I left, and when I arrived home, I called her at 10:15 pm to ensure she was still in bed and alright. All good, she said, but she really wanted to go to the bathroom one more time. I made her take the phone with her, so I could hear everything. She got back to bed just fine. I pressed her to promise me she would not get up again until I got back in the morning. She agreed and we said our good nights.

The ringing of my phone woke me shortly after 3:00 am. I was informed by the manager of the retirement home that my mother had sustained a devastating fall and had been rushed by ambulance to an unknown hospital; she didn't know where they had taken her. The best the manager could figure was she fell sometime between 11:00 pm and 12:00 am, as the paramedics had been with her in her suite for about an hour.

The fall tore a large chunk out of her right forearm, throwing her into the beginning of organ failure, and as well, she was experiencing rapid onset dementia. She was put on oxygen full time, as her oxygen saturation levels dropped when they removed the nasal tube and tried to have her breathe on her own. They determined that Mom went into shock when she fell and had spent a couple of hours on the floor bleeding before she finally found the emergency bell pull in her room. When the paramedics got her to the hospital around 3:30-4:00 am, they contacted me to tell me where she was as I was listed as her next of kin.

The next eleven days were spent with her writhing in agony from the thigh pains. I sat with her every day watching her beat her legs, begging God to take her life, then in the evenings, she "sun downed", experiencing nightly delusions and hallucinations combined with surprising bouts of strength. The morning after her first night with dementia, the nurses came in to restrain her. "It is for her own safety" they said, asking me to sign the consent form as I had her medical power of attorney.

I had been at the hospital with her all night and was exhausted from trying to soothe her as she screamed that she and I had both been kidnapped. She continually begged me to call the police. The nurses walked me out of the room and kindly suggested I should go home for sleep as I was no good to her in my exhausted state. On my drive home, it became necessary for me to pull over to the side of the road as strong emotions roared through my body, shaking me to my core, and I wept from the enormity and pain of the entire situation.

Watching my mother's arms restrained so she couldn't move was more than I could bear. My emotions, bubbling up from the depths of my gut, made it difficult for me to breathe, swallow, or see. As tears flooded my eyes, I trembled as I was tortured by thoughts of the pain that she was going through. Luckily, I was not too far from my daughter's home, so when I calmed down, I drove there to be surrounded in love by my precious family. She and I embraced each other as we both stood crying, me for the mother I knew I would soon lose and she for my pain and her nannie she too would soon lose.

Empathic abilities are strong through many generations of our family, and my daughter could physically feel my pain as I felt my mothers. Those few moments were moments I will treasure till the day I move on from this life. She and I stood holding each other physically and soulfully connected, in support and love for each other. No words were necessary as our souls communed with the pain and grief that we both felt.

The dementia mom suffered continued every single evening, going on until the wee hours of each morning. She would cry out for help as she thought she had been kidnapped and insisted that we get the police to come. She would try to get out of bed, tearing at her clothes, and it left me feeling so helpless, so angry, so overwhelmed with emotions I could barely control myself. It became necessary for me to frequently leave her room to allow my emotions to overflow—emotions I didn't want her to see. Seeing my mother in such excruciating pain, so delusional and in and out of consciousness, was overwhelming for me. It became so unbearable and emotionally draining for me that, God help me, I too begged Him to take her and release her from her suffering.

On July 18th, four days before the third anniversary of my father's death, she suffered a major setback and the doctor called me at 7:00 am to come to the hospital. We had to decide whether to put her on an automatic oxygen delivery system. Mom had signed a "Do Not Resuscitate" order as well as making it clear she did not want any extraordinary measures taken to prolong her life. I immediately called my siblings to let them know of the change in her status. The doctor told us it was only a matter of time.

We discussed the treatment plan and, although it was inappropriate timing, one of my siblings got very angry with me, saying, "It doesn't matter what we all think or feel, you will go ahead and do what *you* want anyhow! *You* have her medical power of attorney and it is *clear* what you want."

This sibling wanted to pull out all the stops, do whatever was necessary to save her life. Not wanting to get further into an uncomfortable confrontation, I reiterated once again what mom had told me she wanted, which was that no heroic measures were to be taken to sustain her life. I know that this upset my sibling and it also triggered a lot of guilt in me through the following days and months that followed her passing.

Mom was quite lucid on her last day, enough so that she was able to spend a little time with us, but slipped into unconsciousness around 7:00-7:30 pm as her oxygen saturation levels dropped lower and lower. She passed away at 11:40 pm.

I sat with my two sisters, my brother, and my husband as we watched our mother take her final breaths. As her breathing grew shallower, I held her hand and she took her last breath. I felt as though the air had been sucked out of the room, and my breathing stopped when she passed away.

I sat alone with her, looking at her beautiful peacefulness, her skin translucent like a porcelain doll. I could not believe this mother who had loved me with every ounce of her being was gone. As I stroked her face, my tears gently fell as I prepared to say goodbye for the last time. As I sat beside her, I leaned down and kissed her forehead, smoothed down her hair, and whispered how much I loved her. I stood, looking down at her one final time, smoothed her soft, delicate hair, turned, and left the hospital room and my beloved mother.

As the business of funeral planning took over my life, I pushed all my feelings aside until that moment when I walked into the church and saw her coffin. The grief overwhelmed like a tidal wave. I collapsed under the pressure of the sobs that shook my entire body to its core.

It seemed fitting that she was laid to rest with my father on the fourth anniversary of his death. They had shared a lifetime together—almost sixty years—and now they were back together again.

I was able to be with both my father and my mother when they passed over. What a gift it was to be with them, surrounding and holding them in love as they took their final breaths. To this day, I continue to be grateful for this gift that they both gave me.

During this time of great loss, Spirit was nudging me in many small ways, but I was not listening. I can see it now as I go back through the circumstances in my life. New interests presented themselves to me as I found myself drawn to researching and learning more about different spiritual and religious theologies. Little did I know at that time that it was Divine intervention taking place in my life, quietly whispering to me, softening me, whispering to my soul in preparation for the evolution and growth that would soon take place.

The years have demonstrated to me, as I have sat at my computer recording all my thoughts for this book, that there are no coincidences. Everything is given and happens for a very specific reason: our soul's evolution and growth. The explosion of growth that I would soon experience was getting closer, but I had one more loss yet to endure.

Our beloved dog, Chelsea, was failing and had been diagnosed with abdominal cancer and it seemed just too much to bear. She had been by our side for fourteen years and we both loved her dearly. My husband suggested I go away on a weekend break with my brothers and sisters. We decided he would stay home with Chelsea; however, we both knew on my return, we would have to make that horrific decision all pet owners dread.

Over the weekend, I enjoyed a one-day riverboat cruise on the Detroit River with my siblings. We toured a few wineries and simply spent time in each other's company. We were still quite raw from these family deaths and, one of my siblings tormented me relentlessly about my newly adopted lifestyle: I had removed gluten from my diet due to my severe intestinal distress. As this sibling had nearly lost one of their grandchildren to undiagnosed celiac disease, I found it especially difficult to endure the many nasty comments.

This sibling was also unwilling to understand or accept that I could be so upset about the impending loss of my wee girl. "After all, it's just a dog," I heard again and again throughout the weekend. When I had been rubbed raw from the constant tormenting, long-suppressed, traumatic memories were awoken and began pouring down on me like a heavy rainstorm.

One week later, we said goodbye to our sweet Chelseabun, exactly six weeks to the day from my mother's death.

Following the death of our sweet pup, I continued to fall deeper into a dark depression. I took up residence in this pit, where I found comfort wrapped in the darkness and in my suffering. I could not see, nor did I make any effort whatsoever to find a way out. During my depression, I was brought to my knees, and I stayed for many months in the suffering that had me wrapped tightly in a thick blanket.

Now, once again dependant on anti-depressants and tranquilizers to get me through, I was unable to see that it had been necessary for me to experience these deaths so I could be reborn. Like the lotus that grows up through the mud to open its glorious flower, it was necessary for me to be covered in the mud of pain and depression so I could awaken to my beautiful authentic light.

How would I have recognized my light had I not experienced my darkness? A star needs the darkness to shine.

It was necessary for me to suffer through these losses, so I could find her, the exceptional woman who had so patiently waited my whole life for me to find her.

The death of my mother hit me very, very hard. The guilt I experienced over not being with her at the time of her fall overwhelmed me as I sunk deeper and deeper into depression.

Over the four years following my dad's death, I had been my mother's primary caregiver, spending copious amounts of time with her. During the last days before her death, I was at the hospital day and night to advocate for my mother's rights. When she passed ten days later, I was finally able to let my emotions flood over me, and this is when the deep guilt surfaced and took over. I blamed myself for leaving her that night: if only I had stayed with her, she would not have fallen.

This became a very dark time in my life. I was coping with not only her death but also the huge hole her death left in my life as my job had been to take care of her. All the love I felt for her now had absolutely nowhere to land. My role as caregiver ended and I did not know how to stop the pain of my overwhelming guilt about her death. My mind replayed this thought over and over in my waking hours: *Mom would have been alive if only stayed with her that fateful night.*

I worried that my marriage was in jeopardy. What few friendships I did have fell away; even family hesitated to call. But I did find comfort in this darkness: wrapped up with my own vicious thoughts, wallowing in pity and feeling so sorry for myself. Throughout this time, I was also managing my mother's final wishes and estate, had many dealings with the government for final taxes, death notices, closing of bank accounts, credit cards. All the while, simultaneously dealing with a sibling who constantly pressured me to handle my mother's final wishes their way.

I was barely staying afloat as I worked my way through my grief and the many, many attempts at releasing the suppressed memories that continued to plague my mind.

By allowing trauma and loss to become the focus in my life, by swallowing my emotions—guilt and shame—and allowing them to overwhelm me, by holding firmly onto my victim mentality, my body was simply unable to cope with any more stresses. So, after years of ignoring the constant and numerous messages my body had given me, my physical and emotional health simply imploded, and I suffered a complete emotional breakdown.

Through all the years, I refused to see my suffering as my messenger or listen to the very strong messages it had sent me.

All the trauma, pain, disease, and loss I had suffered with throughout my lifetime had been my messenger telling me that I needed to explore profound change. Instead, I wallowed in my discomfort and pain, validated by the attention it brought me, all the while wondering what life had in store for me and my future with all this physical pain and mental anguish. These four losses so close on each other's heels were exactly what I needed to shake me awake. So often, hitting rock bottom is what is needed to begin the healing process. As the saying goes, when you hit rock bottom, there is only one way to go, and that's up.

I had a choice to make. I could continue drowning in the pit of darkness I was living in, or I could choose to climb out of the pit. You'll remember so many years earlier I had worked tirelessly to heal my many physical diseases. My mom's death awoke me to the realization that there are three distinct parts to my human self: physical, emotional, and spiritual. I needed to heal my emotional and spiritual self in order for my physical self to be whole.

Intuitively I knew that I must begin deep inner work to heal myself, so I chose to climb out of that pit and begin living and stop simply existing. Over the next few chapters, I will discuss the many methods and modalities I dove into to heal my life.

While I was deep in my grief over these losses, I was totally oblivious to the fact that the Divine was using these circumstances, situations, and losses to soften me for the incredible spiritual awakening and healing that would propel me into a new life just a few months after losing my mom.

> ### Exceptional Woman Challenge: GROWING THROUGH GRIEF AND LOSS
>
> Have you experienced loss in your life? Are you able to look deeply into your grief and the loss to see what lessons or messages are hidden within for your growth? Losses are difficult and soul crushing; however, they are given for your growth and evolution.
>
> I challenge you to take the time to look at any losses you have experienced, even if they were years ago. Begin first with gratitude for your losses, for without them, you would not be where you are today. I understand it seems ridiculous to be grateful for losing a loved one; however, every single loss is given to you to propel you forward, to help you learn what is needed to be exceptional. If forgiveness is needed, forgive those involved, including yourself. These are the necessary first steps in dealing with loss.

Chapter Ten

Coming Home

While I was still experiencing profound mental anguish, my daughter called me one day from a photo shoot she was doing for the yoga studio she frequented. She was doing a lifestyle shoot for one of their yogis. This woman marketed herself as a spiritual intuitive. She told me this woman had shared things with her, things that no one could have known, and talked about me and the loss of my mom. Sebrina said to me, "Mom, you need to make an appointment with this woman to talk to her. It might help."

I went to her website to read about her services; however, I was shocked at what she charged. I told Sebrina there was no way I would spend that kind of money just to talk to her. She re-iterated what Theresa had said to her: "If it is meant to be for your mom to see me, she will come." Finding myself drawn back again and again to her website, reading about this woman and not being able to get her off my mind, two weeks later, I scheduled an appointment with her.

Theresa and I spent close to three hours together during my first appointment. In that time, she explained to me how my mother's life was laid out according to her own contract. I had nothing to feel guilty about in her death as my mother chose how she would leave this earthly incarnation. Her beautiful words and love expressed towards me enabled me to release my guilt. I have often equated our time together as my metamorphosis. She simply walked me to the edge of the cliff and said, "you're ready to fly." Then she gave me the push I needed to use my wings.

Between Spirit gently nudging me over the past few years and then spending that time with Theresa, I felt renewed. I knew I would be taking on a tremendously difficult journey to healing, but I was ready for the challenge. Living how I had been living was no longer working for me, and I was excited to step into this newfound hopeful space I had discovered. She left me with five words that I'll never forget: "Everything is always perfectly perfect."

A few months after meeting with Theresa, we were invited to attend an annual winter solstice celebration. While sitting at the harvest table enjoying our plenty, a woman came in and walked directly over to where I was sitting. She said down beside me and introduced herself to me as Patty.

We spoke at length and I allowed myself to feel all the feelings around the death of my mother. Feeling safe with her, I allowed the tears to fall. She gently placed her hand on my shoulder, and I felt a shock run through my body. It was such a different and unusual sensation, and I asked her what it was. She explained to me that she was a Reiki Master and was channeling energy to me.

From that moment on, the trajectory of my life changed. It was no longer in my hands but in the hands of the Divine, and I felt a knowing deep within me that I had come home.

We talked deeply and for hours about Reiki. It was as if no one else even existed at the dinner party, only Patty and me. I told her that Reiki had been on my list of healing modalities I wanted to explore and what a coincidence that we should meet. She told me she held a Reiki healing circle once a week and invited me to come to it. When the evening was over, we lost touch for a few weeks, but during that time, I began exploring Reiki online, researching what it was and feeling that it was something I would like to study. But would I be able to do it? At the time, I didn't understand that we are all born with healing ability. Think for a moment of any time you have injured yourself. What is the first thing you usually do? You reach for and hold the injury with your hands. There is healing in your hands, and attunement to Reiki energy simply reawakens this ability that we are all born with.

With limited knowledge about Reiki and energy healing, and rather than pay the higher cost of a course with a Reiki master, I decided to take an online course which came with a distant attunement. I studied diligently and a date was set for my distant attunement. At the time, I was volunteering at the retirement residence where my mother had lived, and I was asked to chaperone a group of senior ladies who were going out to dinner and then to see the musical play, *Mame*, at a small community theatre. It had slipped my mind that this was the day I was to be attuned. While we were watching the play, I suddenly experienced a strange sensation on the crown of my head, like little electrical shocks running around. And suddenly, I felt like I had come out of my body and was looking down onto the audience. Instantly I remembered, my attunement had been scheduled and this must have been what was happening.

Shortly after that, I got back in touch with Patty and she invited me once again to the Reiki circle she hosted. As she opened her door to me, she instantly said, "What has happened to you? Your energy is completely different."

That night, during a beautiful Reiki healing circle, I received my first ever Reiki healing treatment from three Reiki practitioners at her home. This was the start of a year of intensive Reiki healing, many shared Reiki circles, and intensive study putting me on the fast track to healing my emotional wounds. I was learning to forgive myself and others while also learning to value and love myself. I slowly discovered the joy of channeling beautiful universal Reiki energies, my Reiki hands coming to life whenever I desired healing for myself or someone else.

During my year of intensive Reiki studying and healing, I also used affirmations constantly. At every opportunity of meditation or healing, I would affirm the emotions I wished to vibrate at and release those I didn't want. For example, during healing, I would consistently say over and over in my mind, "I release anger, resentment, judgement, and self-hate. I embrace joy and peace, acceptance, and love."

Let no one tell you affirmations do not work. Remember, every cell in your body is listening to every thought you think, and in one short year, I moved from an angry, resentful woman full of hate and judgement to one of acceptance of myself and others, planting me firmly on the path of learning to love myself. The journey continues even today as I consistently remind myself of the thoughts I wish to hold. Whenever a negative thought or an adverse reaction to a situation happens, I immediately stop by telling myself *I am choosing* to feel this way. By acknowledging these thoughts, I can instantly replace them with different, more positive thoughts. I also remind myself that the situation I am reacting to is not my problem but the person who created the situation, and then I can release it and move on.

As my heart opened, I knew what it meant to love others truly, authentically, and unconditionally. New and beautiful souls were attracted to me as I quickly learned that LOVE was what I was now radiating.

I learned the value of genuinely loving myself, and I found the love that I felt for others was magnified exponentially.

A few years ago, I was very suddenly struck within unexplained bladder pain, which was diagnosed as painful bladder syndrome and an overactive bladder. The pain was so intense, I shut down. I stopped moving and cocooned into my body, trying unsuccessfully to cope with the pain. After years of trying many different modalities including many prescription drugs to ease the pain, I have discovered and tried a natural solution for my pain and remain pain free today, however I was blessed to learn some very valuable lessons about self-love and self-worth throughout this time.

When we don't take the time for self-care, it is quite natural to fall into judgement and hatred for our bodies, especially when from our perspective, our body has failed us. We judge ourselves for not exercising, for not eating properly, and looking in the mirror becomes difficult. All we can see is our failure to take care of ourselves, which naturally leads to criticizing all our perceived flaws. Because we are not caring for our body—our temple—our self-worth and self-love fall off our radar.

All those years of cocooning within my bubble of pain, as well as a lack of movement, led me down the path to binging and junk-food eating. Self-hate, loathing, judgement, and criticism all came tumbling back into my life. The weight I had worked so diligently to lose a few years prior slowly crept back on my body along with a bit extra.

When I finally gained control over the pain, I decided I needed to challenge myself, so I undertook a virtual challenge to complete the 800kilometre Camino de Santiago. Walking this pilgrimage was something I had for years dreamed about, however, with COVID totally changing our world, I decided instead to virtually cycle the full distance. I began cycling indoors every day, gradually building up my distances to fifteen kilometres daily. Do you know what happened? With the increase in my body movement, my self-worth and self-love also increased. The judgement and criticism I had felt for myself began to fall away as I once again began looking at myself through the lens of love.

Remember the importance of your temple; care for it as you would your child. Place your own self-care at the top of your priority list. Remember what the flight attendant tells you when you're flying: "put on your own oxygen mask before attending to others." It is absolutely impossible to give ourselves one hundred percent to anything if our cup is only half full! If you're not loving your body through your actions, you will find it difficult to unconditionally feel all-inclusive love for yourself.

Studying Reiki intently over four years, I was honoured to achieve the level of Master/ Teacher/Practitioner. This firmly cemented me on my path to share this beautiful gift with others. Through my continued studies at the various levels of Reiki, I could feel deep within myself that I was indeed home, I understood and felt a profound sense of connectedness to the entire universe, a knowing that I am Divine and the Divine is me, together as one in love.

Shortly into my healing journey, I began co-creating poetry. The words started coming fast and furious. There were nights when I was kept awake as the words which downloaded into my mind simply flowed from my pen to the paper.

Today I offer deep gratitude for each and every illness, every abuse, every loss, every disease, as well as my grief and my suffering because it brought me to this point.

Remember, a star needs the darkness to shine.

After I received my Reiki Level III, I spent the following year mastering the art of becoming a Reiki Master. During this year, I also decided to pursue ordination as a metaphysical reverend. Following my ordination, I applied for and received my license as an officiant, offering personalized wedding ceremonies to couples. Following my insatiable hunger for knowledge, I felt led to enrol at the University of Sedona in their metaphysical study program. To date, I have finished my master's studies and exams. Upon completion of my thesis, I look forward to receiving my master's degree.

Through the many years of my journey, I worked diligently to fall in love with me and all of my flawsomeness. I love all the different parts of me—my shadow side, my light side, my too wide hips, my luscious curves, my warrior, my victim, my manipulator, my puritan, but most importantly, my powerful woman energy. Accepting and learning to love myself coupled with an attitude of gratitude consumed me as I began this profound journey towards healing my emotional self, which I knew would lead to truly healing my physical body.

Digging deeper and deeper, I released anger, resentment, and judgement, fully surrendering to my Divine Creator and accepting that everything is always perfectly perfect. I experienced many more relationship losses in those early years, but as those doors closed, I was able to see and absorb the lessons they provided for my emotional and spiritual growth.

And as the saying goes, "when one door closes, another one opens." And there were so many more doors that were waiting to open, full of unlimited opportunities for me. I believe with all my heart that losses, trauma, and difficult situations in life are all gifted for our evolution and growth. If we choose to accept them with grace and in full surrender to our Divine creator, we will see that there is always something else more magnificent waiting in the wings to be discovered.

> ### Exceptional Woman Challenge: USING THE POWER OF ENERGY TO HEAL
>
> This chapter's challenge is for you to look into some form of healing that taps into energy. You might take a yoga class, maybe consider a Reiki session. I offer in person as well as distance healing sessions and you can reach me through my website www.barbaratakeda.com or on social media platforms, Facebook, and Instagram.
>
> Look into Tai Chi or Qigong. They both use the movement of your own body to move energy, pulling in positive energy flow and pushing out negative.
>
> There are a tremendous number of healing modalities available today: Reiki, Therapeutic Touch, Body Talk, BEAM™, EFT, Cranial Sacral, Neuro Linguistic Programming (NLP), Ho'oponopono, Emotional Freedom Technique (EFT) and many, many others. Do your research and find the modality and the practitioner that resonates most with you.

Chapter Eleven

Understanding the Lessons Underlying Loss

There is a saying that "People come into your life for a reason, a season, or a lifetime. When you know which one it is, you will know what to do for that person."

As your understanding of your deep spiritual connection increases, you will realize that everyone who comes into your life is there to fulfill a purpose. Some are there to test you, some are there and will use you, some are there to love you, and some are there to teach you. However, the most important ones are the ones who support and love you, bringing out the best in you.

When someone comes into your life for a reason, they are there because one or both of you needs to learn an important life lesson. When the lesson has been learned, the work is done and the relationship will usually end, sometimes through death, sometimes because they walk away, or oftentimes a situation arises that forces you to take a stand and walk away.

When someone comes into your life for a season, that friend will arrive bringing with them the experiences that you need. Or they might be there to teach you something you have never learned or done. Usually, this friendship brings with it an unbelievable amount of joy, which is real, but only for a season. The intensity of this relationship develops quickly, and it is intense, which is often an indicator that this is a seasoned person. I can relate here to the four "season" friendship losses I experienced. Each of them began with an intense love for each other. It was almost like a honeymoon period, wanting to spend copious amounts of time together, deeply loving each other until we didn't. The losses were abrupt, swift, and cut deep.

We often have that friend that changes how we see ourselves. If your friend was a free spirit, you may have learned not to take yourself so seriously and enjoy life more. They likely provided you with the opportunity to be a little less rigid, maybe a wee bit more spontaneous in life and not quite so anxious about everything. We all go through periods of personal growth, and it can often be attributed to an individual in our life who helped us in becoming the person we were really meant to be.

A lifetime friend will teach you lessons, the things you need to build upon to have a firm emotional foundation. You must accept the lessons, love this person, and use what you have learned in all other relationships and areas in your life. A lifetime friend will weather the storms and the up and downs of friendship but will remain in your life.

The above explanation shows the differences and reasons in the variety of friends, lovers, even family that comes into and through your life. Until such time as you can see and learn the lessons being presented through your relationships, you will continue attracting the same type of person again and again. The lesson is not always learned with one loss, but as you can see with my story, it often comes after many failed relationships. The Universe wants to ensure the lesson is genuinely received and learned as was my case.

The four close friendship losses I suffered all occurred seemingly out of nowhere. Each of these friends and I shared what I thought was a deep abiding love, but when the time came for them to leave, harsh, cruel words were either spoken or written to me and they removed themselves from my life in an instant. It took four losses for me to finally see and understand the lessons that were being provided for my evolution and growth that were hidden within each relationship.

A situation or relationship will continue to repeat until we learn the lessons we are being shown from them.

It had been necessary for me to go through four very similar, very intense relationships and suffer many years of profound emotional turmoil that I might have avoided had I discovered and learned my lesson on the first loss. But the Universe needed to guarantee that I really got it.

Our friendships grew quickly; we became very close very fast, doing everything together, spending copious amounts of time together healing, sharing many deep spiritual conversations. Each of these women came into my life as mentors, and I looked up to them, comparing myself to them, wishing I could have their knowledge, their abilities. They were bigger than life in my eyes, with a large following of clientele who adored them. However, as I progressed in my journey, I could see the cracks forming in the pedestals I had placed them on. And once I saw these cracks, it was impossible to go back to my state of adoration. This became the first nail in the coffin leading to the death of these relationships. Each of these women were energetic healers as I am. We read energy, so I'm quite sure that they felt the change in my energy as my respect for them began to dwindle. This, I am quite sure, is what lead to the demise of each of these friendships.

As a highly empathic person, I attract narcissistic type personalities to me. This type of personality can easily gain control over someone with empathic abilities because of our all-consuming compassion for what we perceive the other person is experiencing. Once they have your loyalty, they begin to gently work at wearing down the foundation of our self-esteem and self-worth. Their language and actions cause us to question ourselves regularly.

A relationship can also break down when the student surpasses the teacher. This changes the balance of power, and often, the teacher can feel as though they are losing control. It is similar to how a parent feels when their young adult child confronts them, desiring more freedom. They may then attempt to suppress you, maybe even use a little gas-lighting to break your confidence. When this happens, it is important to recognize that it is time to move on. Don't allow them to break you. On your healing journey, you need true, honest love and support.

As a giving person who enjoys being in service, I was taken advantage of by these friends. When the balance shifted in our relationship, these friends grew uneasy and that is when the problems began. My husband, the supportive man that he has always been, never said anything to me through these friendships, but after experiencing my second loss, he told me that he and our daughter had been concerned for me when they saw how this relationship had been all give and no receiving on my part. With each of these friends I lost, there was always a gut feeling, a hurt deep down about why it was always me who made contact and not them; however, I continued holding that position of lead planner, always setting up the get togethers, giving and constantly making excuses for why the friend was unable to arrange it. They had young children, I'd say to myself, or they were busy with schooling, full time jobs, etc. I always made the dinners, inviting them and their families to our home, gifting them with many bags of beautiful clothing I was ready to let go of, and often with small gifts for no reason at all.

There were so many red flags that I chose to ignore. On the surface when we spent time together, it appeared they felt great love for me as I did for them. But there was always that little voice deep down, that I chose not to listen to, asking, wondering. Why, I wondered? What was I receiving in this friendship? The hardest part for me was after the loss, I could easily go back and see the gas-lighting, the unkind words that they had spoken in a feigned loving way. It is unfortunate that I suffered four such devastating losses, however, it was necessary for me, in order to learn these lessons and also to ensure they were well established. I now go into friendships much slower, allowing them to develop and grow on their own. I can more easily spot the red flags warning me away from certain people. So am I grateful for the losses—you bet I am!

These difficult losses of friendship were necessary so I could grow into the person I was to become—a person who would go on to help others work through very similar situations. As I look back over these relationships, I can see now that my intuition was giving me messages by way of my discomfort with certain things in our relationships. But I ignored them, feeling guilty for feeling that way and blaming myself for the perceived problems. This is exactly how a narcissist works to create control, doubt, and which creates the ground for that question to bloom—am I good enough? Had I paid attention to my intuition I could have saved myself a great deal of pain, but would I have learned the lessons? I think not.

I will stop here to reiterate: I am worthy ... I am deserving ... I am enough. And my friend, so are you!

If you are offered a beautiful meal, but you can see the food has small shards of glass laced throughout it, would you eat it? Definitely not, and yet we go back to these relationships again and again for the pain, the hurt, the humiliation when we really should be removing them from our life.

Today, I continue to learn and practice receiving, not just giving. I have learned what integrity truly is: it is always doing the right thing, even when no one else is watching. I have learned the importance of remaining humble and staying in humility even as my knowledge, wisdom, and ability to affect and inspire others grows. I have learned to say what I mean and mean what I say. I have learned that ego must never be in the driver's seat when we enter into a healing position working with others. And I have also learned that I will never again relinquish my control to another person.

Once we can sit in a position of seeing relationships as a tool for our evolution and growth, it makes both the gains and losses so much easier to bear. It is imperative to Understand that when you lose, there will be a gain waiting in the wings for you to accept.

Exceptional Woman Challenge: RECOGNIZING TRUE AND AUTHENTIC RELATIONSHIPS

I challenge you today to look into the relationships in your life. Do they satisfy your needs? Do these relationships boost you, support you, love you, or are they discreetly tearing you down, saying hurtful words and taking while not giving?

If the relationships in your life do not support you, hold you up, cheerlead for you, and congratulate and show genuine pleasure at your successes, then maybe you need to take a deep, hard look. If they are not serving your highest good, it may be time to let them go. Maybe, just maybe, it is time to look for a new support system.

Chapter Twelve

Gratitude: The Catalyst that Changed my Life

In 2015, I challenged myself to give gratitude in a public forum for the entire year: all three hundred and sixty-five days. And in doing so, I created a profound change in my life. Was it easy? HELL NO! Challenging myself to give gratitude publicly every day for the entire year, not only kept me accountable, but I found myself slowly moving into a stronger attitude of gratitude with the passing of each and every day. It became easier to find the gratitude in every single breath . . . every single moment . . . every single situation that occurred in my life.

I went on to give gratitude in that same public forum for a full five years—1825 days. This past year, I once again challenged myself to another full year of gratitude. And once again, it enabled me to sit in an attitude of gratitude.

Gratitude has been and continues to be the cornerstone upon which I build my life.

Whatever comes my way, gratitude is and always will be my first thought when I'm working my way through it. Yes, it may be difficult, but there is always something within our losses, pain, traumas, and difficulties to be grateful for. And, when I stop my mind from going into overdrive, when I slow down and shift into gratitude, I always find that thankfulness for every situation. Now when difficulties arise, I no longer ask "why me" but rather, "why not me?" and always, always through the eyes of gratitude, continually searching for the lessons that are being provided for my ultimate growth.

Now when difficulties arise, I no longer ask "why me" but rather, "why not me?"

Moving into an attitude of gratitude *can* and *will* effect tremendous change in your life. When you begin to appreciate what you already have in your life, the Universe will give you that much more to be grateful for. The Universal Law of Attraction becomes more apparent in your life when you are grateful. You attract what you put out, and if you remain in gratitude, you will be given so much more to be grateful for. As the late Dr. Wayne Dyer said, "Be in a state of gratitude for everything that shows up in your life. Be thankful for the storms as well as the smooth sailing. Is there a lesson or gift in what you are experiencing right now? Find your joy not in what's missing in your life, but in how you can serve."

Flip the Script and Make Gratitude the Pivotal Point Around Which Your Life Revolves

There is a verse in the Bible that loosely translated says, "As a man thinketh in his heart, so he is." And Dr. Wayne Dyer expanded on that thought even further with these words, "If you can change your thoughts, you can change your life."

Pay attention to your thoughts and your world, your relationships, and family around you. Soon you will see that what you are thinking *is* creating your reality. If you think loving, grateful thoughts, you will attract loving, grateful people into your life. If you constantly think negative, judgemental, angry thoughts, that, too, is exactly what you will attract into your life.

We are energetic creations, all created from one Divine source of energy. So, it naturally follows that our thoughts are also energetic. Pause for a moment here and think about a time when you've entered a room and you instantly felt something was off. Maybe you felt irritated, or you suddenly found yourself not wanting to stay in that room. Why do you think that is? It is most likely because you are energetically picking up on someone in the room who may be holding negative, angry, possibly resentful, thoughts. Because our thoughts are a form of energy, their vibrations extend beyond our physical body. That is why many people are affected by others' thoughts.

Have you ever stopped to think how everything, and I mean *everything* we see in this big, beautiful world that we live in, began with one single thought? The Wright Brothers wanted to fly like a bird, and today because of that single thought, we are able to cross oceans and fly around the world in jet propelled airplanes and witness space travel in our lifetime.

Alexander Graham Bell wanted to be able to talk to someone in a different location than where he was, and today because of that single thought, we have progressed to being able to speak to anyone, anywhere in the world on a cell phone no bigger than the palm of our hand using wireless technology. Can you imagine what Mr. Bell would be thinking if he could see the progress that has been made from his single thought?

Even the simple, little things that we take for granted every single day, like cutlery, toothbrushes, cardboard boxes, can openers, eyeglasses, pens and pencils, all began with a thought in someone's mind.

I cannot stress enough the importance of paying attention to the thoughts you consistently think.

- Are they negative or positive?
- Are they loving or hateful?

- Are they grateful or constantly wanting more?
- Are they humble or ego based, full of pride?
- Are you constantly judging others and yourself?

What thoughts run through your mind when you see yourself in the mirror, when you look at your body with all of its flawsomeness?

When we judge others, it is quite often because we recognize something in them that is within us, and we are using that criticism or judgement to avoid looking at our own issues.

You can choose to change your thought process. It won't happen overnight, but I promise you, if you devote yourself to changing your thoughts, you *will* achieve it. In his timeless book, *Think and Grow Rich*, Napoleon Hill wrote eleven of the most profound and powerful words ever strung together: "Whatever the mind can conceive and believe, the mind can achieve." I have spent nearly a decade now disciplining myself to think differently, to think loving thoughts about others and myself, to stop judging others and most especially, to stop judging myself, and most importantly to be grateful for every moment, every breath, every "thing."

Here are some tips for flipping your script:

When the thought, "I have to ..." comes into your mind, immediately turn that thought into "I get to …".

When you roll out of bed in the morning, with the thoughts running through your mind, "I have to get up, I have to get the kids up, pack their lunches, I have to get them dressed, I have to get them to school or daycare and then I have to get myself to work, all by 9:00 am." Flip your script as you catch yourself starting to think these thoughts. Instead, say, "I *get* to get up to go to work where I *get* a paycheque that allows me to fill my refrigerator and cupboards with food for the lunches that I *get* to pack for my precious children that I *get* to wake up each morning. I *get* to drive them to daycare or school in an automobile that I most likely paid for with the paycheque from the job I *get* to go to."

You can see from the above example how flipping the words from "I have to", to "I get to" completely reframes the intent and energetic vibrations of your thoughts. This is the difference between a scarcity mindset and one of abundance. Start feeling gratitude for what you have and release the feelings of always wanting more and not feeling satisfied with what you already have. When we begin to feel satisfied and happy with what we have, we will attract more abundance into our lives.

When a complaint enters your mind, replace it with a positive thought. For example, I used to complain non-stop about my pain until I began to understand that, by constantly complaining, I was identifying myself with my pain. I still have chronic pain; however, it is not as intense now due to the numerous changes I have made in my diet, lifestyle, and, most importantly, my thought processes. I still experience days when the pain is stronger, but I re-affirm to myself that "I am in my best possible health today."

When you begin to focus more on what you already have in your life, life will bless you with even more to be thankful for. But if you consistently have thoughts of lack, always wishing for or wanting more, you will continue to live without. These types of people always blame everyone else for their bad luck or misfortune, never thinking for one minute that they are actually the person who created the very world that they are living in.

Thoughts are things!

Do you find yourself triggered or irritated by a particular person? This is a difficult one, my friends, but triggers are often mirroring back to you something within your own psyche that you don't want to look at. For example, if you are being triggered by someone who complains constantly, look back at yourself. Why is their complaining bothering you? Are you maybe a reformed complainer? Or maybe do you martyr yourself by not complaining and then, when you are triggered by this person who is getting sympathy and attention for their complaining, you secretly wish you could get that same attention? Food for thought.

Exceptional Woman Challenge: PRACTICING GRATITUDE DAILY

This is absolutely my favourite challenge, as gratitude profoundly changed my life.

I challenge you to begin giving gratitude on a daily basis. There are so many ways to begin a gratitude habit. Create your own gratitude jar, keep it nearby so you can drop pieces of paper into it with your gratitude written on them. Keep a journal, where you can write your gratitude each morning when you wake, or before you rise from bed every morning, give gratitude for three things. They can be as simple as opening your eyes to another beautiful day, clean clothes in your closet or a comfortable, warm bed upon which to rest and sleep.

I would love to know how gratitude changes your life and would love for you to connect with me via my website or social media.

Chapter Thirteen

Clean up Your Life & Your Space

As your life and your thoughts begin to change, you will find the desire to purge clutter from your life becomes stronger. ***It is difficult to have a clear mind when you are surrounded by clutter.***

I recall shortly after my spiritual awakening, I cleaned out closets and took over two dozen full garbage bags to the thrift store. The clothing and household items were full of things I had held onto, even though I intuitively knew I did not need it any longer. I continue to this day to keep my space free of clutter, free of unnecessary pieces of clothing, books, and plants that are not thriving. And by regularly donating to a thrift shop or homeless shelter, someone less fortunate than me can benefit from my cleanup.

Marie Kondo, author of *The Life Changing Magic of Tidying Up*, writes, "Does it spark joy? If it doesn't, let it go." You can be sure it will spark joy for someone else. There is a common saying: "one man's trash is another man's treasure." I have seen this again and again when I have released something I no longer want. Someone comes to pick it up and absolutely loves it. And an added bonus is that it makes you feel good to give things away to someone who otherwise might not have the means to acquire it.

Feng Shui is a wonderful method that can be used to bring harmony, peace, and balance into your home and subsequently into your life. Here are a few basic principles:

1. Clear the clutter—this will help you lighten up the load, so to speak.

2. Ensure good air quality and light. Air and light are essential for good Feng Shui (called *chi*) energy in your home. Place purifying plants around your home and allow in as much natural light as possible. And where natural light is not possible, consider using full spectrum light bulbs.

3. Define your energy map—read about the Bagua or Feng Shui energy map. There is a plethora of information about Feng Shui online. It will help you to determine which areas of your home are connected to specific areas of your life. For example, in traditional Feng Shui, the southeast corner of your home is connected to the flow of money energy into your life. Keep this corner free of clutter. Maybe add a jade plant. A water feature creates a never-ending cycle that represents money flowing.

4. Understand the basic five Feng Shui elements of wood, fire, earth, metal, and water. Using these in your home creates balance and vibrant energy in all the different areas. For example, if you wish to attract more prosperity, you would use the elements of wood and water in the southeast area of your home. To improve your health, place lush plants in the east area of your home.

5. Research your Feng Shui Birth Element and use the element to create a home that nurtures and supports your energy. My birth element is air, so I have created open spaces in my home with renovations to remove unnecessary walls as well as using mirrors to reflect light and create the illusion of airiness where there is none.

6. Be mindful of the quality of the energy in your home. Does it feel good, is it able to move freely, or is it stagnant? Pay close attention to the Feng Shui trinity that is deeply connected to your health: your bedroom, your bathroom, and your kitchen.

Ensure that your gardens and home are neat, free of clutter, and that there is a free-flowing path to and from your front door. Having clutter in the pathway blocks the energetic flow. Don't keep recycle bins, old gardening pots, or shoes around the doorway.

As I said earlier, get rid of clutter, clean out your closets, basement, garage. And once you get them cleaned out, don't let them accumulate more clutter. Keep your plants, both indoor and out, free of dead or rotting leaves. This introduces bad energy into your space. By embracing the right energies in your home, you can keep your home healthy and happy.

Exceptional Woman Challenge: CREATE HARMONY IN YOUR LIFE

This challenge is to encourage you to purge what you no longer need from your home. What do you have taking up space around your home that you no longer really need? Bag it up and donate it to your nearest thrift shop or homeless shelter. I don't expect you to purge from your entire home. Begin slowly and be gentle with yourself. Begin by taking everything out of one closet and go through to see what brings you joy when you hold it. If it's a clothing closet and you haven't worn an item in a year, time to let it go. A quick tip in helping you discover what you wear often is to turn all the hangers in the opposite direction, in other words, backwards to how you normally hang them. Then when you take something out to wear, put the hanger back in the regular position. This can quickly tell you which items you wear the most and which items you do not wear.

I also challenge you to do some research and reading on Feng Shui. It is a fun and fascinating way to create harmony within your home and your life. There are many simple books on Feng Shui that you can pick up to help simplify its principles for you.

Once you've completed your homework, take one area of your home and apply these principles to it.

Chapter Fourteen

You CAN Rewrite Your Life

I spent many years locked in anger, resentment, and judgement of not only myself but others. As a result, I attracted the same type of individuals back into my life. Years of soul-searching and many tearful episodes face-to-face with myself in front of my mirror brought me to a place of acceptance. It allowed me to drop my judgement of not only myself but others. I am now comfortable in my own skin, and I completely own my luscious flawsomeness. I can truly say, "I live my life with inner and outer joy." And this all started with discovering and allowing myself to feel love for myself. I can say that I now live a life of abundance because I found deep and unconditional *love* for myself.

I am no longer defined by my story. Do you remember that little girl who sat weeping silently on her bed feeling unworthy, unloved, not good enough, hating herself and living her life wrapped in anger and resentment? Well, she is still here, but I have embraced and loved her. I love her, I forgive her, and I now re-parent her with love, kindness, and compassion. I have released my judgement of her, and in coming back home to me, she has found her magnificent light. Through learning how to live in the present rather than the past, I live a more mindful life. Remember, the past is only a memory, and the future is not yet ours.

Now, instead of negative thoughts about myself, I feel a deep connection to the Universe through deep understanding and profound gratitude for the people, situations, circumstances, events, losses, and illnesses that were provided to show me what I needed to learn in order to grow.

Profound change is possible; it is within your grasp. Only ten short years ago, I wrote in my journal, "I need to learn to love myself, create my own joy and not depend upon others for my happiness."

To be present, you must work on releasing the past. The past is, in this present moment, simply a memory, and it cannot hurt you any longer, unless you choose to let it.

If you continue to hurt from the memories, it is because you are choosing to allow that hurt.

It may be a painful, difficult memory, but you must come to an understanding that it can no longer hurt you. Holding onto the past hurts no one but you.

You must move into a place of forgiveness for yourself and for those who hurt you or that you perceived to have hurt you. Once you can genuinely forgive yourself and them, it becomes easier to give gratitude for the difficulties you went through. Remember, in order to recognize the light, we must experience the darkness. I repeat: a star requires the darkness to shine.

Anyone else involved in what you perceive as a traumatic event has likely moved on, and while you continue to hold anger and resentment, it does not affect them in any way whatsoever. However, the anger that you continue grasping onto will create blockages in your body that sooner or later will show up as disease, maybe physical, maybe mental, but I guarantee you, it will eventually make an appearance. When thoughts of past situations, events, trauma, or pain arise in your mind, begin slowly replacing them with something more positive and uplifting. I realize this is a difficult ask, but with time and practice, you can do it. This book is my testimony to what I have done in healing my life. By accepting and following the Exceptional Woman Challenges, I know you can too. By picking up and reading this book about my healing journey, you have already demonstrated that you are at a place in your life and ready to begin the healing process.

Buddha said, "holding onto anger is like drinking poison and expecting the other person to die." The other person does not feel any effect of your lack of forgiveness; however, it most assuredly will affect you. If you find yourself full of anger or feeling resentment, you are dwelling on your past pain. In effect, you are still living in the past, and as time goes by, your perception of that pain changes. We increase our reaction to it. We will talk to anyone about it when they take the time to listen. This cements our victim mentality firmly in place as we consistently spin the stories in our favour.

How can you expect to turn to a new page in the chapters of your life, if you cannot close the book on the chapters from your past?

If you spend a great deal of time worrying about what may come, or you find yourself suffering from anxiety or panic attacks, once again, you are not staying present. Your life is ordered, and there are two dates you cannot change—the date of your birth and the date of your death. Nothing will be changed by your obsessing over "what might happen." If it is meant to be, it *will* happen. So why worry if you cannot change the outcome? The future is not yet yours; you only have this very moment. Excessive worry tells the Universe that you cannot and do not trust your journey.

The beautiful Hawaiian Ho'oponopono prayer is a simple yet beautiful healing modality. This is a Westernized version of an ancient Hawaiian problem-solving process created by Dr. Hew Len and popularized by Joe Vitale. The Ho'oponopono prayer helps us with repentance, forgiveness, and change within its four simple lines:

I love you ... I am sorry ... Please forgive me ... Thank you

The four parts of the prayer work on the assumption that we are each fully responsible for everything in our lives. If someone else is suffering, it is from the memories we are holding onto. Remember, we are all one, created individually from one energetic source—God. So, what affects you, affects me. The super or subconscious mind is how we are directly connected to our Divine Creator. Our soul includes both the conscious and the subconscious mind. Joe Vitale and Dr. Len, from their book Zero Limits, say, "when we come into this world, we come from the void. Our identity originated in the void. To return to our self I-dentity, we must work to regain the void, a state of zero. We do this by clearing away our memories, our habitual ways, and our automatic responses. Ho'oponopono is a petition or prayer to Divine Intelligence to clear or change our memories back to a state of zero".

By speaking the four parts of the prayer, we are cleansing ourselves, which in turn begins affecting those surrounding us.

1. "I love you." This is for the memories. Use this again and again because even if you are not conscious of problems, it will help to clear those memories and allow a clear channel of inspiration to flow from Divine Intelligence.
2. "I'm sorry." This is your acknowledgement of responsibility for having created, accumulated, or accepted the memories replaying and causing trouble.
3. "Please forgive me." This is a subsequent petition for having caused the trouble.
4. "Thank you." By feeling and expressing gratitude, you are requesting that the memories be changed, neutralized, and released.

There is a plethora of information and many spiritual leaders out there willing to help you on your journey. I do, however, strongly suggest that you be mindful when choosing someone to work with. Look at the ways in which they interact with the community of which they are a part. Are they well respected and well loved? Do they remain humble even though they may have a large following? *This is really important!*

If they have many followers, there is always the possibility that their ego "may" actually be in charge, not their higher self. The higher self wants only to serve. The ego, although it also wants to serve is also searching for validation from serving, always looking for others to build them up, giving them a sense of importance. This is not to say that every healer with a large following is driven by ego, but it is very, very easy to allow the validation and applause to feed it.

Often, when we begin working with healers, coaches, and mentors, we frequently elevate that person to position of guru, looking at them as though they are next to God. You must remember, they too are a soul journeying this lifetime, the same as you. They are human just like you, with human foibles just like you. Do not place them on a pedestal or elevate them to a position higher than yourself. They are on a healing journey also, just like you. When that pedestal develops cracks, it is a devastating blow to a newly healed soul still evolving and growing. I can speak from experience here, as I did this many, many times, with mentors in the early days of my healing journey. I was developing my skills but could not see them due to my lack of confidence, always looking up to them with the thought, "if only I could be like them, if only I could have the knowledge they do, if only I could have the large clientele like they do".

Work with someone who embraces humility, but who leaves their ego out of the equation. And ensure they always follow a strict moral compass. Is their healing practice based on the revenue they bring in, or are their clients their priority?

When I have a new client come to me, we sit and chat for a wee bit before I progress to the healing. It is necessary that they feel safe with me, comfortable to share with me and allow me to place my healing hands on them. When we finally get down to the Reiki healing session, I take a moment to guide them into deep breathing, and, in that moment, I look into their beautiful face and fall in love with their soul. That is how I know when I am channeling beautiful universal Reiki energies: it will be infused with the love one soul feels for another.

Reiki energy healing helps to bring you back to the remembrance of who you were when you came into this world, encouraging your body to let the healer within come forward.

If you are truly open and committed to energy healing, the results can be spectacular. Energy healing will give you a totally new perspective as you open your mind to infinite possibilities, to the oneness of this world, to your oneness with our Divine Creator. We have all been created through energy. We are energetic beings, but as we grow, through a lifetime of programming and conditioning by parents, siblings, friends, teachers, religious mentors, advertising, media and what we choose to read, we forget who we truly are.

Marianne Williamson wrote: "Our deepest fear is not that we are inadequate. Our deepest fear is that we are powerful beyond measure. It is our light, not our darkness, that most frightens us. We ask ourselves, who am I to be brilliant, gorgeous, talented, and fabulous?"

My question to you, dear reader, is who are you *not* to be brilliant, gorgeous, talented, and fabulous?

Exceptional Woman Challenge: ACCEPT THAT EVERYTHING IS ALWAYS PERFECTLY PERFECT

My final challenge to you is to apply what you've read in this book to your life. Begin slowly and be prepared for difficulties. I'll break it down into simple points here.

1. Reframe the thoughts you think regularly. Remember, you are creating your reality with every thought you think.

2. Adopt an attitude of gratitude. Be grateful for everything you have right now, including everything you've been through—difficult, painful, and otherwise.

3. Use affirmations regularly.

4. Begin to love the person you are. Use Louise Hay's 21 Day Mirror Challenge. Then watch as all inclusive, unconditional love for you is mirrored out to all those around you.

5. Always look for the lessons within every situation. Even when someone is triggering you, there is a lesson to be learned. Remember, too, that when you are triggered, they are mirroring back to you something within you that you are refusing to see, heal or deal with.

6. Surrender your life to your higher power … God … The Universe. Accept that everything is always perfectly perfect. And finally, release what no longer serves your higher self.

7. Self care is NOT optional. Incorporate one small, simple act into your life today. Go to bed a few minutes earlier. Prepare yourself a beautiful meal. Have a bubble bath fragranced with beautiful essential oils. Light candles and play soft music.

Chapter Fifteen

Exploring Emotions Through Poetry

Following are a few pieces of the unedited poetry that I wrote during my early years of healing. These came from a very raw, emotional place and it's my desire that they touch you in those same deep places, healing the wounds that you carry and give you a glimmer of what is possible for you!

I am beginning this chapter a little differently by challenging you before you read it.

EXCEPTIONAL WOMAN CHALLENGE

I would like to challenge you to explore your own journaling. Take the time to be still, be present, and allow the pen in your hand to take the lead. Simply write anything and everything that comes into your mind.

Journaling is a wonderful way to keep a record of your healing journey. I have journaled for years and I am amazed when I go back and see where I was, even as recent as last year. This beautiful journey of healing is ongoing, each day bringing with it new revelations, more growth and evolution, more forgiveness, more gratitude, more love. I cannot tell you that it won't be painful; however, it will also be rewarding.

I encourage you to adopt journaling as a daily habit. During the early days of your healing journey, writing down your emotions, your thoughts, and feelings are critical to your ability to successfully work through them and then release them.

Buy yourself a beautiful journal and pen. Be extravagant, as having something beautiful in your hands will encourage you to make this a daily habit.

In the beginning days, simply open your journal, take your pen in hand and sit in a quiet space. Allow the words to come to you. Whatever thought crosses your mind, jot them down. After doing this for a while, review your entries. You will be so surprised with what you have written when you go back through your musings.

Now buckle up, dear reader, and hold on. Because …..

"THIS IS GOING TO BE AMAZING!!!!

Be Still

Everything is chaos, as it swirls around me, like a maelstrom that threatens to pull me down

Into its depths where I will be lost

My soul in agony, cries for release from its' physical constraints, "Let me take the lead", it cries

"And if you follow, I will bring you home"

"I see my destination", I hear the spirits call to me, "If you will let me answer, I will show you the way"

I must leave the chaos behind and pull myself from this turmoil, which threatens my very existence

The physical dis-ease which plagues my every waking moment cries to be released from this body

But then I sense a stillness and peace, somewhere deep within my soul

A deep thirst cries to be satisfied and I reach out to grasp that which cannot be confined

Its' size is beyond my comprehension, no borders, no boundaries - real but unreal

I must possess this feeling

Now, everything else drops away, my soul is suddenly released

The chrysalis that once held this butterfly has broken open - I am released

I have won my freedom - I can fly

To a place of peace, to a place of love, to a place of complete contentment

Were they always there? In front of me, but unseen by these eyes

I have arrived - I am love and peace - I am complete contentment

I am everything that was, is and will be. I have learned - to be still

Coming Home

The pain of the past, simmering just beneath the face she exposed to the world

Always there, churning and bubbling, destroying her self-esteem, her morals, her thoughts, her abilities.

Deeper and deeper they went until she couldn't recognize them any longer

What happened to this woman? What hurts, what pain, what grief?

That left her wanting health, happiness, freedom from the pain.

How deep must she dig to release this pain? Can she find what she seeks?

She experienced abuse, she experienced death, she experienced the sting of cruelty from a friend, the bite of hate within her family.

All working together to create that fertile ground for every negative emotion

Anger, resentment, self-loathing, judgement, bitterness, envy.

This girl was good for no one

But then one day, her whole life changed, she was brought to the edge, but could she take the next step?

What was waiting beyond - forgiveness, acceptance, self-love, humility. All within her reach.

Was she ready to release the past?

The cloaks of grief and depression were wrapped tightly around her, they had her locked within their grips. They comforted her, they eased her pain, protected her from the world.

Was she ready to drop these crutches? No.

But deep within, she knew she must let them drop from her body as leaves must drop from the trees in autumn.

Shifting, awakening, changing at her core, releasing ego, piety, anger, resentments.

The list was painfully long

The pain was moving upwards and outwards – it was breaking the surface, wearing her down.

Reliving and reminding her of the horrors.

How low her vibrations were; but now they were rising.

She felt the difference in her soul, she loved, she laughed, she was embracing the wholeness of life.

Reiki became part of her journey, introduced to her one winter solstice night.

She felt the pulsing energy and knew she was home.

Her searching was over - a new spiritual life was opening to her.

The fear of death was gone, replaced with peacefulness.

The horrors of a cruel God, replaced with a Divine source of unconditional love.

She pondered her lives, previously and yet to come.

How many lives had she lived? How many more would she live? What gifts had she given?

What gifts had she to offer the world?

A new life was hers - was within her reach

The hurts were all gone, replaced with unconditional all-encompassing love.

How did she exist so long un-aware? Living but not alive

Reiki had brought her joy, and she would forever be grateful for that winter solstice night.

When she felt the energy in that hand on her shoulder, waking her up, changing her core, filling her up.

She had come home

<u>Healing</u>

Her hands gently touch my face, the hands of this beautiful soul sister

I feel the energy flow, slowly at first, then faster and harder

My body and soul cry out for this energy

Dark, primal thoughts assault my senses, ancient memories intrude

As past lives float in and out of my consciousness

On a crystal, glass lake I drift - I see a woman in a white robe

I am her and she is me

I am floating, I am rocking, I am pulsing, the energy is soft, the energy is hard, it is gentle, it is everywhere.

My dreams are constantly interrupted, as my body tries to clear the blocks

I will myself to control my body's movements, but they are stronger than my will

Muscles jump and my torso spasms

"Let the energies flow," I hear again and again

Now I sense her hands moving through my chakras

They are on me, in me, going through me

Our hearts beat as one as her soul lays gently on mine

And the energy opens, releases, and clears the blocks throughout my body, sweet, pure love is what I sense

Flowing through the hands of this woman I love

I have known her before, we are bound through our life experiences

The love is pulsing and beating to my very core,

To the part of me that wants to stay hidden

It is awoken, crying out "heal me"

I am a goddess, I am divine, I am a healer and I have healed through many, many lives

I see again the woman in white robes,

We are one - a healer, a priestess. She walks through my mind

I am becoming who I was born to be, but first I must embrace myself - all of me

My spiritual, my emotional and my physical, my feminine self, my sexuality

Release the guilt, the deep dark parts of me, the parts I keep secret

Acknowledge, accept and release my shame, and lovingly accept all of me, forgiving myself

As I continue the healing journey, towards this magnificent woman,

In love with herself and her life

And always remembering I am worthy

Connected

I am a woman, a goddess. I am the universe - I am divine, I am loved and I am love

I am life, I am everything.

I share love unconditionally - no expectations.

My heart is open and laid bare on the table of life.

Moments of introspection are precious to me as meditation opens a new world re-connecting me to my divine feminine. To my radiance which was my birthright

We are one connected by our hearts.

Gaze deeply into my eyes and you'll find yourself there - at the core of my being, in the depths of my heart. There you reside, my love.

We are powerful, the creators of life. In our woman's belly, we nurture this life.

Embrace your beauty, love your woman's belly, this place where life begins and miracles happen

And accept.

I embrace my oneness with the Universe and the Universal divine power.

I am divine - we are divine, as one we can change the world.

Home at Last

I am but a pilgrim journeying in this world travelling through my life's experiences.

As my days gently flow together.

From a place of love, I came - To a place of love, I will return.

Learning lessons and growing as I continue my journey.

My energy flows with high vibrational frequencies. Other souls on the same frequency flock to me. We've known each other long, long ago

I chose this journey before my birth to achieve my full potential and fulfill my destiny.

I yearn for the day when I'll return home, safe into the arms of loved ones gone before.

Oh, the joy I'll embrace when I experience unconditional love, surrounding me, lifting me up, sweeping me along in blissful peace.

No pain, no worry, no need for words. We'll exchange our love from heart to heart.

I will finally be home

All is Well and Perfect

The healing road is long and rough,
A winding road with many turns
And seemingly insurmountable mountains along the way
Will I ever reach the end?

I thought I had healed after years of hard work
My chakras had opened, in harmony they spun
My heart wall came down, emotions released
I was strong, but then a trust was broken,
As was my heart.
Like a sail with no wind, I was empty
My trust shattered like fragile glass
How do I let go, how do I move on?
Cutting the emotional cords that bind us together
This loss of friendship and energy
Cut deeply into my soul

Can I trust I will have that love and bond again?
Dare I let myself allow someone else in?
If I invest my all, will I be shattered again?
Suddenly I knew, everything was different
My chakras were closed
Energies didn't flow as they had,
Physical pain had increased
In vain I searched for the path to come back

Should I let down my guard, share my emotions
What if I'm hurt again?

But then in the quiet of my meditations
I hear a voice speak softly to me
"Remember dear heart - this is a gift
Embrace the pain, feel the pain, process the pain
And be open - there are lessons to be learned

Leave the hurts of the past behind you
And move into this moment
Use the hurt to strengthen your resolve
To stay true to your path
Your destiny is as a powerful healer
Sharing this gift with many
You will endure heartbreak and pain
And suffering is part of the path you must walk
Take the time to learn to heal yourself

Acknowledge this and know you will heal
And in this knowledge, you will become stronger
Allow the flow of energies to heal you
And open your chakras
Rest in the knowledge
That all is well and perfect.

Gratitude

As a droplet in still waters ripple ever outward
Growing larger and larger, so my gratitude grows
As I wake, it is my first thought
Each breath - each second - each moment
I breathe in acceptance and breathe out gratitude
In rhythmic cadence with the beat of my heart

What is this life I have chosen?
What lessons must I learn?
My soul cries out to its creator
As a babe cries out to its mother

Touch me with your spirit,
Fill me with your strength
Let me feel the power of your greatness
Teach me humility
I feel spirit move within me,
Because I am awake
The magnitude of spirit overwhelms me,
I cannot speak
As I sit quietly in reverence - and realize - I am.

Additional Resources

Marianne Williamson – www.marianne.com

Marie Kondo – www.konmari.com

Joe Vitale – www.joevitalehooponopono.com

Tosca Reno – www.toscareno.com

Dr. Wayne Dyer - www.drwaynedyer.com

Gratitudes

My dear husband who has been my rock through all the years of illness and continues to support me in this journey through uncharted territory.

My mother and father, without whom I would not be.

My beautiful and amazing children and grandchildren, whose very presence in my life fills my lungs with breath and my heart to overflowing with love, pride and tenderness.

Dr. Wayne Dyer, whose beautiful book, "The Power of Intention" completely changed my life and my thinking.

My editor Akoshua (Jackie) Brown. There are not enough words in the world to express my gratitude for this woman and what she has done for me through this process. The way she was able to pull so much more from me than I ever thought possible and her uncanny ability to turn my thoughts and words into brilliant writing.

Two very dear friends, Errol Knight & Trev Lewis, without whom I may not have risen to where I am. Their unwavering love and support for me was the wind beneath my wings. Their cheerleading for me led me to stand up and speak in front of crowds, enabling me to inspire others to embark on their healing journey.

Theresa Marcotte, the amazing spiritual mentor who held my hand and walked me through the beginnings of my healing and also enabled me to release my guilt.

My mentor Alvin Brown, who taught me that every single thing resides in this very moment and by mastering myself and my thoughts, I am able to stay present and appreciate the blessings within this moment.

And lastly, I must acknowledge those who have come through my life, offering lessons by triggering me, hurting me, bullying me or controlling me. Once again, I am grateful for each and every one of these people, as they too helped mold me into the exceptional woman I am today.

About the Author

Through many, many decades, Barb Takeda showed up as not enough in her life, living most of the time with debilitating chronic illness and depression. Suffering through many losses, she found her purpose and her passion which brought her through her dark night of the soul to find her light. Soul searching led her to a profound understanding that every step, every loss, every trauma, every circumstance was the Divine plan given for her soul's evolution and growth. Through full surrender and acceptance, she was able to overcome her victim mentality and be the victor of her story.

Barb is a best-selling author with her first co-authored book, "The Courage to Change", published in 2019. As well, she is an inspirational speaker, Reiki Master/Healer/Teacher, spiritual mentor and empowerment coach. She is also a reverend and wedding officiant.

Under her company Soul Full Expressions, she created an intimate event for women, "An Exceptional Woman", bringing in guest speakers to encourage and inspire women to unleash their exceptional! She motivates and empowers women using the spiritual tools and principles that she employed to find her way out of her darkness.

Barb lives in Southern Ontario with her husband and fur baby and is a mom to two children and grandmother of four.

You can reach Barb through her website www.barbaratakeda.ca or on social media, Facebook and Instagram under her name.

Authors Note

"You are worth it"

www.ingramcontent.com/pod-product-compliance
Lightning Source LLC
Chambersburg PA
CBHW072055110526
44590CB00018B/3186